D1202769

A LAYMAN'S
INTRODUCTION
TO CHRISTIAN THOUGHT

Books by *James Kallas*
Published by THE WESTMINSTER PRESS

A Layman's Introduction to Christian Thought
Jesus and the Power of Satan
The Satanward View: A Study in Pauline Theology

A LAYMAN'S
INTRODUCTION
TO CHRISTIAN THOUGHT

by JAMES KALLAS

THE WESTMINSTER PRESS
Philadelphia

Copyright © MCMLXIX The Westminster Press

STANDARD BOOK NO. 664-24854-3
LIBRARY OF CONGRESS CATALOG CARD NO. 69-16919

PUBLISHED BY THE WESTMINSTER PRESS®
PHILADELPHIA, PENNSYLVANIA
PRINTED IN THE UNITED STATES OF AMERICA

Dedicated . . .
    . . . to Darlean, partner in pleasure and pain

37426

PREFACE

WE are drowning in a deluge of despair. The breast-beaters and the pessimistic palm-wringers are decrying the death of God, declaiming the decline of Christianity, assuring us that the day of the church is past and that we are now living in the post-Christian age.

Voices within and without the church lean on us, all the day long advising us that we are now living in a secularized society, that religious foundations are eroding, that traditional concepts are now outmoded and irrelevant, that Biblical language is obscure or—worse—unimportant to modern man. The publishing market is flooded with best sellers informing us either that Christian doctrine is hopelessly archaic and pathetically antiquated (J. A. T. Robinson, *Honest to God*) or triumphantly trumpeting, with all the elastic vitality of a man who has for the first time discovered indoor plumbing, that cities are nice, that we have moved into the bright promising dawn of a liberated society in which our environment can be examined anew and appreciated for its own merits, our vision emancipated from the blinders of earlier traditionalism (Harvey Cox, *The Secular City*).

The whole movement is nonsensical, pathetically ill-grounded on untenable premises. Those who argue that Biblical language is offensive are of course correct. The Biblical language *is* offensive. But not because it is archaic, antiquated, intellectually indefensible, or incomprehensible. It is offensive precisely because it *is* comprehensible! The Christian message is held at arm's length not because it is intellectually insulting. There is nothing inherently illogical or philosophically irrational in the dogmas of the church. Able minds of every century have always been able to distill the basic meaning from

Christian truth and make it palatable and presentable in the thought categories of their society. Rather, the Christian message is held at arm's length because it demands commitment, surrender, allegiance, the very qualities that the skeptics and critics of our day, and of every day, refuse to give it. When all the verbiage of battle is stripped away and the essential issue laid bare, it becomes consistently clear that what is usually lacking in the critic of Christianity is not intellectual information but existential surrender. The Christian message is offensive, in our time as it has been since its beginning, because it demands that man see himself as a sinner. *That* is its offense. Not that it is couched in obsolete terminology, not that it represents an antiquated world view, not that it is philosophically absurd or empirically unsupported, but that it demands surrender, commitment, allegiance, an acknowledgment of need, a confession of weakness, an acceptance of help from powers outside ourselves. In that sense, Christianity is a humiliation. It makes us confess that we are not self-sufficient. Such a view will always arouse resistance.

Those who argue that we are living in the post-Christian age and that the church's day is done, and who support that accusative affirmation with a barrage of statistics indicating the relative decline of Christianity in respect to the overall population growth, let them be reminded that Christianity has *always* been a minority! Jesus had only twelve disciples. One was a traitor, and the other eleven ran away. We do not take the spiritual temperature of the church via statistics. The church is what it has always been—the body of Christ. Despite all its human flaws and failures, it remains the instrument of God. And it shall not fail in its purposes, because it is upheld by powers greater than man's thin arms or small hat size.

These apostles of pessimism who tell us that the church is dying must be looking at some church other than that which I see! All I see are signs of ferment, of feverish activity, of virile action, of passionate concern. For example, to be topical and activist, there is not a single major denomination in the United States that is not in one way or another seeking to face up to and ameliorate the racial crisis of our time. To say that the effort is belated is to echo the obvious. But to deny that the effort is being made is to be either blind or dishonest to God. Or, another example, to be theological and reflective, I see not only an intensified and widespread concern for activist programs but also a desire to know basic theological truths and teachings upon which intelligent action can be based. I see in countless local congregations a renewed and ever-increasing concern for adult Bible studies, for a reexamination of and a renewed appreciation of doctrinal emphases now recognized once more as vitally significant for intelligent action in an increasingly complex world. The church *is* alive, seeking to be servant of its Lord.

It is in an attempt to enter into and aid this growing renewed interest in Biblical studies that this book is written.

J. K.

California Lutheran College
Thousand Oaks, California

CONTENTS

INTRODUCTION

A FEW words of explanation (or warning) as to what kind of book this is are probably in order. As the title indicates, this is a book of Christian theology. But even that needs further definition, because there are different kinds of theology and there are subdivisions within Christian theological thought. Speaking broadly, there are three kinds of Christian theology —apologetic, systematic, and practical. That is, there is an attempt to *justify* Christian thought, defend it and show its reasonableness (apologetics). There is the attempt to *explain* it, sum up its inner essence (systematics). And there is the attempt to *apply* it (practical theology, or ethics).

This book is *not* apologetics. Our purpose here is not to defend Christianity as a philosophical system, showing its inherent reasonableness. Apologetics is an attempt to prove, by logical evidence, the existence of God. Apologetics, by examining the world about us and by drawing deductions from the evidence thus gathered, seeks to prove to men of reasonable mind that God, in fact, does exist. This is the avenue of approach of at least one major stream of Christian thought, that followed by the Catholic Church since the days of Aquinas. An introduction to Christian thought taught or written by a Catholic begins not with the Scriptures but with natural law, with an observation of and an analysis of the world in which we live, an analysis that seeks to convince men of honest mind that God does exist and that proofs of that fact can be garnered from nature.

For example, to give but one illustration of this approach, apologetics would point to the very existence of the creation as proof that there must be a Creator. If I find a beautifully tooled gold watch lying on the beach, the very existence of that watch proves to me, a logical man open to the evidence of reason, that there must be a watchmaker. The pounding of the surf, the shifting of the sands, these impersonal forces of nature could not have made a watch. There must be a watchmaker somewhere. The existence of the creation, a beautifully tooled intricately meshing cosmos where all the parts fit and the seasons flow one out of another, proves, says apologetics, that there must be a creation maker, God, somewhere.

But this line of approach has weaknesses, serious weaknesses. In the first place, if the existence of the watch proves that there must have been a watchmaker, what does the existence of the watchmaker prove? Obviously, that someone or something had made him! The argument is inconclusive. It really doesn't prove anything.

Secondly, growing out of this, there is the further obvious fact that these supposed "proofs" really don't prove anything at all. The arguments *are* inconclusive. That is seen in the fact that for centuries reasonable men have been exposed to this kind of logic and *still* have not believed in the existence of God. If these were proofs which truly demanded that reasonable men in examining them would be forced to believe in the existence of God, then how do we account for the fact that many reasonable men of every generation have not been convinced? As Immanuel Kant showed, logical argument is nothing but propaganda for defending a prior prejudice. Just as you can logically prove the existence of God, so also you can logically disprove the existence of God. Protestant theology, therefore, has widely abandoned this apologetic approach to Christian theology, and in that Protestant stream I swim. This is not a book of apologetics.

Furthermore, even if, for the sake of argument, we assumed that apologetics could do what it claimed to do—prove the existence of God—it does *not* follow therefore that Biblical faith is consequently created. Biblical faith is not intellectual assent to a series of academic propositions, it is not nodding your head yes to the idea that God exists. Biblical faith is instead personal commitment, heartfelt trust, the ordering of one's life in accord with that insight. And *that* is a matter of the will, not of the mind per se. The Bible itself insists that "even the demons believe" in the existence of God (James 2:19), but they do not live accordingly, they do not bend in obedience before him.

Apologetics, therefore, might be of some value to someone already in the faith, assuring him that his faith was not irrational or anti-intellectual. But apologetics is unable to create in and of itself Biblical faith. Thus our argument here is not *apologetic* theology. I would hope that some of the arguments developed in these pages can and will strengthen one's realization that the Christian faith is not romantic fiction or religious fabrication, but is instead reasonable in its own right and able to answer many of the problems of humankind with more incisiveness than does any competing philosophy or faith. But if I do serve such an apologetic purpose, it will be only as a by-product, not as a primary purpose.

This accounts for the bluntness of my beginning. Central to the Christian proclamation is the announcement that Jesus deals with sin. I have not begun, as would an apologist, by trying to prove the existence of sin, by trying to explain its origins or analyze its history in human affairs. I have simply assumed that it is a fact and have gone on from there, trying to explain the different Biblical ways of comprehending it. In other words, my purpose is *systematic*, an attempt to *explain* Biblical teaching, not to defend it or to prove it.

The same general remarks hold true for the other area of Christian theology, ethics or applied practical theology. This too, like apologetics, is outside the purpose of this book. I am not trying to imply, of course, that ethics or application is irrelevant. On the contrary, I have tried to show, in at least a few places, how the vertical (the Christian confession of the Fatherhood of God) has implications for the horizontal (the brotherhood of man). That is, I would hope that somewhere in the course of this book the reader will clearly see that the way he acts must flow out of what he believes. But again, any emphasis on ethics is a by-product of our purpose. Our primary purpose here is neither apologetic nor practical theology, but rather systematic theology—an attempt to explain without prior philosophical justification and without consequent ethical application what the mainstream of Christian theology has always believed in respect to such issues as the nature of man, of sin, of the work of Christ, and so on.

So much for the *kind* of theology we will treat here. A few more explanatory comments on the word "theology" itself. The word comes from the two Greek words *theos* and *logia*, which mean respectively "God" and "a word about, a study of."

"God" stresses the *divine* side of theology. In the very word itself there is the insistence that the study is a revelation, a divine disclosure. The study at hand is not human fabrication or invention, but it is *given*, of God, containing a divine dimension. This fact fits in with and helps explain the point just made, namely, why Protestant theology at least has never stressed natural law and has in general abandoned apologetics as a proper approach to Christian theology. We cannot prove with human evidence and observation what was given by a higher authority. Even to try to use apologetics is in the minds of at least a few Protestant theologians akin to idolatry. It is an attempt to make God's existence and message dependent upon human knowledge. This is what lies behind the historical Protestant conviction, "The Word Alone." The final arbiter is not what man thinks but rather what God says. This is *theo*logy, a divine revelation, a given which we neither support nor create but before which we bend.

Theology, then, is more than mere human thought. It is divine. This means that in one sense I read the Bible even as I would read Plato or Shakespeare. I use all the tools of good academic investigation. I must learn the history of the times that produced the people. I must know and understand the original language and thought patterns of the people who penned those words. I must understand the problems and currents of that far-distant past which swept around them and often overwhelmed them. I must read the Bible seeking to hear the aspirations and hopes of fellow human beings long since

passed from the scene. But I read with *more* than that in view.
I recognize that, unlike Plato and Shakespeare, this is *not* just
human insight but divine revelation: *God* has spoken in these
pages, and man must obey. That is what the word *theos* in
theology stresses.

But, as already hinted, like Jesus himself who had a dual
nature, Christian theology has a human side as well. *Logia*
tells us that this is a word about God, a word by man. Theology
is a man-constructed system. The Bible may be a divine revelation, but it is a divine revelation *given through men,* and theology is the classification of Biblical insights into logical order
by men. In other words, theology is fallible. It is open to error
and misapprehension. Christian theology may be a summation
of divine expression, but it is a *human* summation of that expression and, as such, subject to error and correction. We are
not saved by our theological systems but rather by the reality
to which those systems point. Theology is a signpost. A signpost is not without value. It points to something permanent,
eternal. But it is only a signpost and no more. Theology is always incomplete, always in need of restatement, a human con-
struction with all the limitations which that implies.

Another thought on this subject. Theology may be limited,
but it is, as *logia* implies, a *logical* system. What I mean is this:
theological thought hangs together; it has an inward unity that
welds all its parts and pieces together. All too often the unini-
tiated looks at theological studies as if they were but a series of
unrelated propositions laid woodenly side by side. All too often
theology is understood as a Roman numeral order of study, an
outline designated by I, II, III, as if we had a bundle of independent axioms not organically interrelated but only mechan-
ically succeeding one another. This is not so. Theology *is* logical, it is cohesive, its parts fit together. The proper imagery
is not that of a Roman numeral I, II, III order of study but
rather that of a spoked wheel. There is a hub, a starting point,
a given center, from which all the spokes extend and upon
which they all depend. Ideas in theology are interdependent.
They grow out of and depend on what has gone before, and

they in turn produce other ideas. Given one truth, that man is a sinner, other truths, such as that Christ is the Savior from sin, grow out of it. That is, the fact that man is a sinner and the fact that Christ is Savior are not independent ideas; they are intrinsically and inseparably welded together and cannot sensibly stand apart like isolated Roman numerals. Or to put it differently, the *way* you define sin is going to determine the way in which you grasp the significance of Christ's work. This will, I hope, become clear as we move through our book.

I begin by trying to show that sin can be defined in three different ways: as rebellion, as guilt, or as bondage. Whichever definition is accepted as the hub will determine in advance how all other doctrines are formulated and framed. It is precisely this fact (and this is one of the major theses of this book) that sin can be defined in three different ways which goes on to determine the fact that we have three mainstreams in contemporary Christianity—the Catholic tradition, the Pentecostal or Baptist emphasis, and the Lutheran or Calvinistic stream. Since there is this logical interrelatedness, this interdependence of the spokes on the hub, this can be a *short* book. Once the inner genius or essence of one of the specific streams of Christianity is grasped and truly understood as the formative principle of that denominational emphasis, it is no longer necessary to develop *every* doctrine, *every* dogma. Instead, the thoughtful reader ought be able to proceed on his own, seeing how the point of departure, the hub, is going to inform and fashion all consequent doctrines.

Finally, on this subject, since theology is a *human* study, we must openly recognize and freely admit that we never completely succeed in laying aside our human biases. We all have presuppositions, things we take for granted and never even argue for, assumptions which color all that we say. Even when we struggle to do so, we never completely succeed in being purely objective. My bias is not only that I am a Protestant, but even more than that, I am a specific brand of Protestantism, a Lutheran. As this book unrolls and I discuss the differing denominational emphases of Catholic, Calvinist, Baptist, and

Lutheran, I will probably inevitably, even if unintentionally, cast Lutheranism in the most favorable light. This means two things. On the one hand, I hope that I have never been totally unfair and not too often inaccurate in my attempt to characterize faiths not my own. On the other hand, I hope that the reader will make the allowances I perhaps have been unable to make, and compensate for my prejudices in favor of Lutheranism by introducing his own in favor of the other faiths discussed.

Chapter One

THREE VIEWS OF SIN

For I delivered to you as of first importance what I also received, that Christ died for our sins in accordance with the scriptures." (I Cor. 15:3.) "He himself bore our sins in his body on the tree." (I Peter 2:24.) "To him all the prophets bear witness that every one who believes in him receives forgiveness of sins through his name." (Acts 10:43.) Any one of these verses, or any one of dozens of others just like them, serves as a simple summary of Christianity. Jesus' life and death and resurrection have something to do with overcoming sin. The first thing to do, then, is to define sin.

Speaking broadly, sin can be defined in three different ways. In the first place, sin is *rebellion*. This is probably the oldest Biblical idea of sin. Adam is in the garden, shaking his thin little fist at the heavens; God has given him an order, "Do not eat of the fruit of this tree," and Adam is rebelling, "I *will* eat of the fruit of this tree!" Sin is rebellion, obstinate resistance, a refusal to do what God commands; it is the arbitrary rejection of the command of God, the refusal to hear any other voice or bend to any other will than our own. Hostility, pride, obstinacy —call it by whatever name you will, but by any name it is always the same: sin is rebellion, a refusal to put God at the center of one's life. Paul calls it enmity, the Old Testament calls it stiff-necked and hardhearted, and Jesus speaks of an evil and adulterous generation, stoning the prophets, spurning the Word of God. Sin is rebellion—pride, hostility, self-centeredness, the arrogant rejection of the Creator by the creature. This is one way in which the Bible sees sin.

But it is not the only way. The Bible also speaks of sin as *guilt*. Now, rebellion and guilt are related, for rebellion produces guilt, but, though related, they are not the same thing.

Guilt is the consequence of rebellion, the stain that remains even after the act of rebellion has ended. There is the sign on the wall, WET PAINT—DO NOT TOUCH. I touch. That is my rebellion. But when I am done touching, when the act is ended, my hand is soiled. That is my guilt. The consequences remain, even after the rebellion is gone. I break the laws of health. I am a drunkard for forty years, ruin my liver and wreck my life. After forty years I turn over a new leaf, stop rebelling. Do I get back the forty years or renew my liver? Of course not. The consequences remain even when the rebellion is gone. And the Bible calls this consequence of the act, as well as the act itself, sin. The Bible calls it uncleanness, defilement, pollution, a dozen different things, and the whole sacrificial system of the Old Testament came into being as an attempt to wash away this uncleanness, this guilt. Rebellion produces guilt, they are related, the one flows out of the other, but, once produced, guilt stands in its own right as an entity to be dealt with. All law, not just Biblical law, recognizes the difference between these two. If a man commits murder, he has rebelled against the laws of society. If this man repents, sets aside his rebellion, cries out, "I'll never do it again!" does the judge let him go free? Of course not. Even if the judge could peel back the top of the man's head, look inside, and be absolutely certain that the man was sincere and never would rebel, commit murder again, *still* the judge would not let the man go free. He would not, for the man is not only a rebel, he is a *guilty* rebel. His *guilt* as well as his rebellion must be dealt with, and dealt with it will be, either through execution or through long years of incarceration in prison. Guilt, then, is the second Biblical way of looking at sin.

But there is yet a third way in which the Bible speaks of sin. In the first two, sin is seen as something that man does or creates, something for which he is responsible. It is either an act, rebellion, or a consequence of that act, guilt. But in either event sin has to do with an *act*. This third view sees sin not as an act but as a *condition*, sin as bondage. Sin is *bondage*. It is slavery, helplessness, being overwhelmed by forces we can neither cope with, control, nor even comprehend, under the influence of evil malignant powers that determine our deeds. Call it what as you wish, but always you end up in the same place: sin is not an act of man but rather a condition in which he finds himself. The most eloquent elaboration of this motif is found in that cry of despair by the apostle Paul who insists, "I can will what is right, *but I cannot do it*" (Rom. 7:18). Then twice in the same context (Rom. 7:17, 20), Paul tells *why* he cannot do the good that he wills but does instead the evil: "It is no longer I that do it, but sin which dwells within me." Paul might flunk Freshman English, for he is redundant, he repeats himself—but he certainly is emphatic! And just how emphatic he is the original Greek makes even clearer, for there he speaks of sin with the definite article, "*the* sin." He speaks of it as a living thing, an invading enemy, a force that has moved in and taken possession, an enemy over which he has no control. Sin is a condition, a condition of bondage, subservience to forces we cannot resist.

Now that we have defined the three Biblical views of sin— rebellion, guilt, and bondage—another point must be made, and this point must be absolutely clear or else you will never be able to understand Biblical thought! These three views are *not* three different ways of saying the same thing! They are *different* things! They are even, if you will, contradictory things, mutually exclusive things. In one instance, sin is an act, something for which man is responsible. In another, sin is a condition imposed on man against his will, something for which he is not responsible. These things are contradictory. The Bible speaks in opposites. Just how or why this can be is a point we will develop in another chapter. But for the moment, presuming on evidence I will give later, I insist only on this: that these three views of sin *are* separate, that they insist upon separate things, that they point to separate and independent realities. Sin *is* rebellion, *is* guilt, *is* bondage, and all three have to be allowed to stand alone, as facts in themselves, each of them primary, each of them fundamental, and each of them Biblically valid, able to be supported or authenticated by a multitude of Bible verses.

One of the greatest dangers to proper Biblical understanding is trying to make one of the three primary, reducing the other two to secondary, dependent consequences. Do that, and the Bible will remain forever a closed book, its meaning beyond you. Take rebellion and insist that it alone is primary—guilt and bondage being its consequences, conditions which flow out of that primeval act of rebellion—and you have not explained Biblical thought, you have perverted it. Or, in the other direction, take bondage and insist that it comes first—that first we are in a condition of bondage and out of that condition come acts of rebellion with consequent guilt—do that and once more you have not elucidated Biblical thought but confounded it. Each of these three things, though in one sense contradictory to the others, must be allowed to stand on its own feet, for each of them points to one of the realities hiding behind that blanket word "sin."

This brings us, then, to a fundamental fact of Biblical thought. Biblical thought is dialectical or paradoxical: it is able to hold opposites together in tension. It is able, without embarrassment, to say two different things, insisting that both are true. And both *are* true, even if not consistent! There *is* a sense in which I am rebellious—responsible and rebellious. I wake up in the morning and I resolve: "Today is going to be different! Today my wife and family are going to see that their husband and father is something other than an ogre! I am going to be kind, be good, let them know that I love them!" I resolve to be a better man. I am *not* going to rebel, to hurt, to be petulant and abusive! And in the very resolving, I am verifying the fact that I do not have to be that way! I *can* be better; I do not need to be rebellious. But that night, alone, when the family is asleep, I wet my pillow with my tears and I cry out again: "Good God, what got into me? Why did I do it? What kind of malignant monster am I? Why did I make them weep once more?" My high resolves, my lofty aspirations, my decisions to do better—all of them were for nothing, and I am reduced to despair. We always hurt the ones we love. Always—unwillingly yes, but always. And in that fact is the truth of human nature. I can will what is right but I cannot do it.

These are opposites, but though opposites, both are true. I am responsible, and my abuse of that responsibility is rebellion, rendering me guilty. I am called to account, stained by my bad acts. But I am also, all too often, aware of the fact that I am a plaything of impulses and mad desires over which I have no control. I am in a condition of bondage, rendering me helpless. The liturgy of one of our Christian churches summarizes that paradoxical fact in a marvelously compact phrase when it is confessed every Sunday morning, "We poor sinners confess unto thee that we are by nature sinful and unclean, and we have sinned against Thee by thought, word, and deed." "*By nature* sinful and unclean"—bondage, slavery, a nature we are born with, stuck with, cannot shed. "And we have sinned . . . by thought, word, and deed"—rebellion, perverse and pervasive rebellion, permeating everything we think or do.

Chapter Two

TWO VIEWS OF MAN

THIS chapter is an enlargement of the last one, a look at the same coin from the other side. Even as sin can be looked at in three ways: rebellion, guilt, or bondage—or maybe, better, in two ways: as an *act* of rebellion resulting in guilt or as a *condition* of bondage—so also man must be seen in contradictory terms. Man is free and responsible but simultaneously helpless and enslaved.

We are responsible, we make decisions. To be a man is not to be a robot or a telephone pole, a mechanical apparatus devoid of choice. To be a human being means to be able to decide, and anything less than this is less than true humanity. A mongoloid baby, or a baby born with brain damage, or a mentally retarded child unable to decide or think for himself become tragically less than human beings in the fullest sense, only thin shadows, a gray mockery of what human life is supposed to be. Every moment of true human life is filled with the necessity of decision-making. I wake up in the morning and I have to decide which of my two neckties I will wear. I choose what to wear, what to eat, where to work. I do not have to live in the heat of Arizona or the cold of Minnesota—I can go where I want, do what I choose. I did not *have to* marry the woman I live with; I *chose* to do so. Man is free, self-determining, responsible, called to account for the things he does and the way he is.

But true as all that is, there is another side to things. There *is* a sense in which I am helpless, determined, my life spelled out for me by forces I cannot alter or correct. When I was in college, I wanted to be an engineer—until I took a course in differential equations! They say that inspiration is 99 percent perspiration. Well, I perspired all over the place. I really worked, and *still* I could not master differential equations. That ended all my hopes of becoming an engineer! My mind simply did not work that way. I tried, I honestly tried, but my mental apparatus simply was not put together in that way. I was limited, determined; academically, engineering was impossible for me, and my college transcript of grades proves it. Or take another example. Have you ever heard of a 105-pound all-American fullback? I haven't! A kid born with a little body like that—a fact over which he has no control—can dream all he wants and perspire all he is able to, but the simple inevitable, irrefutable fact is that he is forever determined, athletically determined, his sporting career spelled out for him by forces he can neither create nor control. He might be a great golfer, but a fullback never. Now, we can understand and accept it when someone speaks this way of being determined in athletics or academic life. No problem is caused intellectually, because the evidence is too conclusive. But as soon as someone says we are determined *religiously* or *ethically,* we throw up our hands in horror and dredge up all those foreboding words such as "predestination" and cry out, "Unfair!" Cry out or not, the fact remains. We *are* determined! There is a sense in which my fate and my actions are not in my hands. Side by side with the insistence that I am a responsible, decision-making person called to account for my actions stands the countertruth that I am determined by forces over which I have no control, that my life is spelled out by forces I cannot resist. And both of these facts are true. Opposites, but both are true.

I remember that once I saw a picture of a young mother on the front page of a newspaper. You could tell from the photo that she was on the edge of nervous hysteria and physical collapse. The caption under the picture made clear why. In her own broken words the story was told: "I don't know what got into me . . . the baby was crying, crying . . . I was only going to spank him . . . I don't know what got into me . . . Oh, God! Give me my baby back!" She had killed her own child. And if we only cluck our teeth like hens and pass judgment, if we fail to see that the same demonic forces lurk within each one of us, waiting for their opportunity to break loose and destroy us, then we are in greater danger than that mother, for we have never seen ourselves for what we are. Ground into our very fiber is a malignant dimension of the demonic, threatening everything that is dear to us. We *do* always hurt the one we love. What about that story of the motorist on the highway who kicked against his flat tire until he broke his own toe! We *do* always hurt the one we love! There *are* times when we are over-whelmed, carried away, blown by the blasts of personality's winter, tragic victims of dreadful foes without face or form. Law recognizes this. Psychology recognizes this. We speak to-day of the youngster who is a "compulsive" delinquent—com-pulsive, compelled, *unable,* to be anything but a delinquent—of a weeping mother with a dead child, of a motorist with a broken toe. To deny it is to be an ostrich. But it is equally absurd to go from that truth to the other extreme and insist that *every* lawbreaker or tirekicker is an innocent victim of irresistible forces. The law *does* say, "Guilty." And the psychia-trist does reason and argue with the disturbed, pleading for the proper decision. *Both* are true. Opposites must be held together in tension. Man *is* free, responsible, called to account. Man *is* determined, helpless, often a slave.

The whole dialectical or paradoxical picture can be put into a different frame. Instead of saying that man is helpless or free, we can say that man is good or evil. Or better, he is both. Good *and* evil, simultaneously, at one and the same time, man is *both.* In the language of the church, man is born in the image of God —good; and is sold into the bondage of the devil—evil. *Simul iustus et peccator,* "Simultaneously a saint and a sinner."

The problem with the philosophers is that they insist upon being consistent; they refuse to hold opposites together in ten-sion. They always stress one side or the other, saying that man is good *or* evil, one or the other, failing to see that he is both. The French Enlightenment said that man is good, a noble crea-ture, pure and in himself undefiled. Man's errors and mistakes were thrust on him from the outside, a product of his environ-ment, the contamination of his companions, the result of the

society in which he found himself. Now, just how his companions got evil, or how his society became contaminated if
man was basically good, is a problem the Enlightenment never
got around to explaining! But insist they did that man was
good. Rousseau spoke of man as a noble savage, pure and undefiled, a high-minded creature. Spurn society with its ills, return to nature, live under the arching cathedral of the heavenly
vaults in the pristine purity of nature, and that pristine purity
will be yours! On this side of the Atlantic, James Fenimore
Cooper wrote his romantic novels of the Mohicans and the
Deerslayer, and his point of view was precisely the same: man
was good, noble, undefiled. The Indians would capture an
enemy and then give him a furlough so that he could go home
and say his good-bys and then return to be executed! Man is
good, a creature of honor, and he will not betray his word once
given.

But at the same time that the Enlightenment was hymning
the glory of noble man the Marquis de Sade (from whose
name comes the word "sadism") was dipping his pen in vitriol
and insisting that the basic nature of man was to rape and to
murder. Man was an animal, a bestial evil animal, and you did
not know man until you knew that! Man lived to inflict pain,
to cause suffering, to create anarchy and chaos! Always, within
man's philosophical structures, only one pole is given, only one
side of the evidence emphasized. Always it is an either/or—
man is good *or* bad, but never both.

Communism as a philosophical system insists that man is
good. "Give as you are able, take according to your need." That
is the basic starting point of Communism. It assumes that I am
good. Since I am a good man, if I have a full wallet and see my
neighbor starving I will open it up and share what I have, help
him out, lift him up. In theory Communism promises that the
state and the police will wither away, no longer needed once
common ownership of all things is achieved, because restraints
will no longer be needed. Once I am co-owner of all things, my
greed will evaporate, my desire to grind my neighbor's nose in
the dust will disappear, and the police will no longer be needed,

because I will do what is right. Communism has no sense of sin, no conviction that man is basically evil, perverse to his core, with greed ground into his being.

Plato felt the same way: man is good, self-determining; show him the right way to walk and walk that way he will. Just show him the proper path to pursue and pursue it he will. That is why education was so important for Plato. Man had to be taught, but once taught, he would do what was right, for enlightened self-interest and innate goodness would lead him along the proper route. Although this idea is as old as Plato, it is as up-to-date and modern as Dr. Spock. Spock's whole approach to baby-raising revolves around the same basic view of man. Man, even a baby man, knows what is right for himself and will go that right way. So, if the baby cries, feed him; if he wants his own way, permit it. The entire modern emphasis on permissiveness is rooted deep in the philosophical conviction that man is a noble creature, intrinsically good.

But the other side is also picked up and elaborated by some. Schopenhauer, the apostle of pessimism, the German philosopher, as legend has it, starved himself to death in front of a full table, because he could find nothing worth living for, no redeeming quality in man worth preserving. Nietzsche cried out that not only was God dead, that there was no vertical absolute, but also went on to insist that there was no horizontal absolute either. If there is no God, if God is not my father, then my neighbor is not my brother. The superman philosophy—the survival of the fittest, dog eat dog, the strong over the weak—came into being, and this is not wrong, this is just the way life is, and man had better learn to live with it. Alongside Plato there is Posidonius and Sophocles, and alongside Spock is Edgar Allan Poe. The conviction that man is evil, determined, overwhelmed by demonic forces that he cannot resist, is as old as the affirmation of the basic goodness of man.

Man *is* evil and man *is* good, and no one-sided evaluation of man that stresses the one pole while ignoring the other is ever going to be complete or accurate! And it is *only* the Bible, among all the diverse systems of human thought, that has the courage and insight and audacity to proclaim that *both* are true, simultaneously, of each of us. The opening chapters of the Bible speak of God's creation and of man within it, and the one word repeated over and over again is "good." "And God saw that it was good." Then he made man ("Let us make man in our image"), and man is good, noble, a creation of God, a reflection of his goodness, so says the Bible. Yet in another place the Bible can turn right around and insist that "the whole world is in the power of the evil one" and that man is a fallen, evil creature, a slave of demonic powers, and we are, all of us, "children of the devil." Behind that poetic imagery of the Bible, behind that metaphorical language which sees man on the one hand made out of the dust of the earth and on the other hand filled with the breath of God, there lies the *only* comprehension of man that is complete and accurate. Man is not good *or* evil, helpless *or* free—he is both! Here the philosophers fail, for they make the part the whole and miss the point. Only the Bible is comprehensive, for man is both good and free, both evil and helpless, because sin is both an act and a condition.

Chapter Three

THE PERSON AND WORK OF CHRIST

IN the opening sentences of the first chapter, I insisted that Christianity can be summarized by saying that Jesus deals with sin. We have defined sin, and now we turn to Jesus—who he is, what he did, his person and his work.

HIS PERSON

The first thing to say is something so obvious that I almost feel absurd in saying it. It is this: Jesus was a Jew, and those who first believed in him and wrote about him, as well as those who wrote the Scriptures that preceded him, were also all Jews. But obvious as that is, it has certain implications which are all too often overlooked. We have to know something about the Jewish language, about Jewish thought patterns, because that language and those patterns are different from Greek views, and whether we always realize it or not, we think today like Greeks and not like Jews. So we have to know what the differences are in order to make allowances, to put ourselves into the proper place to see as they who first wrote about these things saw. We have to pull the plugs out of our minds and let our Western, our Greek, preconceptions flow away, and we have to think like Jews.

The place to begin is with the facts of language. The basic building block of the Hebrew language is the verb. The simple three-consonant verb is the starting point of their whole structure of thought. All the other parts of speech—nouns, pronouns, adjectives, everything—are built upon the verb. For the Greek, on the other hand, the elemental unit is the noun. In the beginning was the noun, and all other parts of speech depend on it. The Hebrew thinks in terms of acts, deeds, works.

The Greek thinks in terms of essences, substances. This one fundamental difference is extraordinarily important; its results are stupendously far-reaching. It has affected everything that the Hebrew or the Greek has thought and believed. The Hebrew begins with God *in action,* a living, doing God. The Hebrew asks "What has God *done?*" The very first line of the very first book of the Bible shows God in action: "In the beginning *God created* the heavens and the earth." No self-respecting Greek could ever have written that! The Greek would have to begin, not by defining what God did or does, but rather by defining who or what God *is!* What is his nature? his essence? Only when that is determined can the Greek draw conclusions as to God's acts. Two of the oldest of the Greek philosophers, the pre-Socratic Thales and Heraclitus, argued as to what was the primeval substance, the material from which all other things were made. One said water, the other said fire, but far apart as they were, they both agreed that one had to begin not with action but with substance, not with work but with person.

This fundamental difference of thought orientation shows up in the creeds of the church. The church began as Hebrew and became Greek, and the switch of nationality is reflected in the alteration of creedal language. The oldest creed is the Apostles' Creed. Legend has it that the apostles were sitting around one Sabbath afternoon, and Peter began, "I believe in God the Father Almighty!" One of the others chimed in, "He was the maker of heaven and earth." And then a third added his article, "I believe in Jesus Christ, his only Son, our Lord." Each of the apostles then contributed his own clause, building on what went before, and when all were done, *voilà,* the Apostles' Creed was complete—hence its name, the *Apostles'* Creed. The story is not true, of course; it is only pious legend. And yet it does make a good story. It shows, in its own way, the antiquity of that creed. Even though its final form was not determined until much later, the roots of that creed go back to the apostles, to the *Jewish* apostles. The point is that in that Jewish-orientated creed, the person of Jesus is spelled out in verbs. Verb forms, participles, are used to describe who Jesus is. "*Con-*

ceived by the Holy Ghost, *born* of the Virgin Mary"—those verb forms are an attempt to describe his divinity. He was not sired by any human father, he is more than man, he was born of a virgin, conceived by the Spirit of God himself. In exactly the same way, his humanity is also described with verbs: "*Suffered*" under Pontius Pilate, "*crucified*," "*dead*," "*buried*." Always, in Jewish thought, the emphasis lies on the verb, on an action, past or present or future, but always on an *action*.

Compare that to what is found in the later creeds, compiled or composed when the church became Greek. Then, in confessions such as the Nicene Creed, the emphasis has passed from verb to noun. It is in terms of substance, not action, that Jesus is described. For example, in the Nicene Creed, Jesus' divinity is no longer simply described in terms of participles; instead, nouns are used. "God of God, Light of Light, Very God of Very God, . . . *being of one substance* with the Father."

Incidentally, to return to a point that we raised earlier and promised to treat later, it is because Biblical thought is Jewish, because it deals with *verbs*, that the Bible is paradoxical, that it is able to hold opposites together in tension. As long as a person is thinking in terms of verbs, acts, he can always and easily think in terms of opposites, for people act differently at different times. The way I act in front of the Internal Revenue Service man when I am called in to verify or defend my income tax return is quite different from the way I act when dealing with my son or some other subordinate! Sometimes we even act differently in front of the *same* person. How about that neighbor of yours? One day he comes over all smiles, finest chap you could know—he wants to borrow your lawnmower. Next day, *he* gets called before the Internal Revenue Service man and he is so angry he has to take out his fury on someone —on you! So there he is, throwing garbage over the fence! Totally unpredictable—one day smiling, the next day a bear! But it causes no problem as long as you think in terms of verbs —then opposites *can* stand side by side, since people *do* act differently at different times.

But if once you begin to think like a Greek, you must be consistent. Opposites are not allowed to stand. Substances do not change; they are always the same. Water is always water, which may be hot or it may be cold, but always eternally two things are true of it: it is liquid and it flows. That never changes. And don't bring *ice* into it! That is *ice*, and not water, as far as Greek thought is concerned! Substances do not change: fire is always hot and fire always burns.

Because the Greek philosopher thought in terms of substances, he opened the door to modern science. Substances obey rules; they are always alike. There are certain unalterable rules at work in the universe that never vary. That is the way the Greek thought, that is the way the modern scientist thinks, and that is the way we think. If we go into a chemistry lab today and perform an experiment, we get a given result. If we go into the lab again tomorrow and perform the same experiment, we will get the same result—at least, we *should* get the same result! If we do not, we assume that our measurements or observations were wrong. We simply assume, because we think in terms of *substances* as the bedrock of all reality, and since substances always act the same way under the same circumstances, that there must be the same result.

But that is *not* the way the Hebrew thought! He did not think in terms of essences but in terms of actions. He believed in a living God who was not bound by unalterable rules. God was a living God who was able to rip into history and bring forth the unpredictable, radically reversing all the expectations of reason. By every standard of human reasoning, by every norm of political science and military logistics, who should have won the struggle between Moses and Pharaoh? That barefooted fugitive from the eastern Arabian deserts, armed with a stick and a memory of a burning bush? Or Pharaoh, the mightiest temporal power of his day? To ask the question that way is to give the answer: of course, by all the unalterable rules of human measurement and observation Pharaoh should have won! But he did not! He did not because he was dealing, not with a chemical axiom, not with an unalterable equation of human logic, but with a living, plunging God who was sheer will, not bound by any rules, who could do as he wished! *That* is why the Hebrew was never a scientist! Not because he was mentally incapable of observing certain general truths in nature and not because he was unable to apply those observations to his own situation, but simply because he was convinced to the depth of his being that there was One who was outside the rules, God!

If the ancient Jew went into the chemistry lab and got a different result from that arrived at yesterday, he could never be sure whether he had measured wrongly or whether God had intervened! The Jew simply was not a scientist. The way he looked at reality would not allow it. He did not think in terms of substances acting by rules but in terms of actions, and actions can vary. Incidentally, without developing it, this is why the entire Science vs. Religion quarrel is just a little bit absurd. Those who would pit the Bible against science are ignorant of the fact that the two are not in opposition; their swords never cross. They are looking in opposite directions, understanding all of reality from radically different starting points. Religion deals with God, with God *in action.* Science deals with substances and their immutable unalterable nature.

But let us return to our point, the person of Jesus. Once we have grasped this fundamental orientation of Jewish thought, that it stresses not nature but action, we are in the proper position to understand how the Bible speaks of the *person* of Jesus, who he *is.* In a word, the Bible, because it is a Hebrew book, really does not care much about, really does not deal with, the question of *who* Jesus is or what is his substance or nature. Rather, it deals almost exclusively with his work, what he *did!* The perplexed cry of the disciples, "Who then is this, that even the wind and sea obey him?" (Mark 4:41) is never answered! The agonizing problem of the later Greek church, confronted by the paradoxical fact that Jesus was confessed as both human and divine, almost foundered on that fact. How could he be both? Human is human, and divine is divine. They are two opposite substances or natures. How then can Jesus be both? How can contradictory substances be harmonized? The Bible gives no answer to how it can be, for the Jew was not interested in how substances can be melded together.

The whole horrendous history of the Greek ecumenical councils, and the creeds hammered out on the anvil of Greek thought, eventually proved nothing, nothing in the sense that anything was ever explained. All that the creeds ever did was to say, negatively, what the church did not believe! Heresy after heresy was rejected. Adoptionism, Docetism, Ebionism, Arianism—all those heresies which subordinated his divinity to his humanity or his humanity to his divinity, rejecting the one side in favor of the other, calling him human *or* divine—all were rejected. The church never really did explain how he could be both! It eventually had to content itself not with explanation but with proclamation: he *is* both! And that is the way it will *always* be. You cannot force the Bible into areas it has never entered. You cannot make it answer questions about which it is unconcerned. You cannot twist it into giving an answer to the Greek question about the essence or nature of Jesus when what it really speaks of is the Hebrew proposition of the work of Jesus.

The upshot of this extended discussion is simply this: if you want to find Biblical evidence indicating that Jesus is both human and divine, you have to expect two things. First, you have to recognize that there are next to no Scriptural passages which deal with that question in precisely that way! You can almost count on the fingers of one hand those passages which clearly and explicitly speak of the *person* of Jesus, who he *is*. John 20:28 is one such passage. Here, Thomas, confronted by the risen Lord, seeing the nail holes and the scar of the spear thrust, cries out, "My Lord and my God!" He calls Jesus "God." Romans 9:5 may be another place where Jesus is flatly called God. I say "may be" because the Greek language here is ambiguous. Everything depends on where you think the period, the end of the sentence, should come. One possible translation is: "According to the flesh, is the Christ. God who is over all be blessed for ever." Another equally possible translation, just as reasonable on the basis of the Greek text, is: "Christ, who is God over all, blessed for ever." There are a few other passages —not many but a few, such as the first verse of the Gospel of John, or some Pauline passages, such as Phil. 2:6 or Col. 1:15— that you might be able to lean on. But in actual fact, you have to recognize that the evidence is limited, and even that limited evidence does not seem to be so much concerned about *who* Jesus is as about *what he does and did!* Thomas calls him God because he sees the nail holes. Jesus is able to overcome death! Who can conquer death but God alone, the source of life? Paul speaks of Jesus as the "image of the invisible God" simply because he is convinced that Jesus is the most powerful personality ever to invade human history, master over the "principalities and powers" whom he has defeated, having "made a public example of them, triumphing over them" (Col. 2:15).

The second thing to bear in mind, then, and this grows right out of what was just said, is that the student who wants Biblical evidence about *who* Jesus is—human or divine—really has to look, not for statements about Jesus' *person*, but rather at descriptions of Jesus' *actions*. It is there, in his acts, that the Bible writers make clear who Jesus is!

For example, as we just saw, it is when Thomas sees that Jesus is able to overcome death that he calls Jesus "God." That truth is always in front of us in the pages of the Bible, for it is on the basis of what he *does* that the Bible writers are trying to indicate who he *is*. Look at Mark 2:1–12. Here, Jesus, confronted by a paralyzed man, does an astounding thing. He announces that the man's sins are forgiven. Immediately the audience explodes in consternation. The scribes start to mutter and say: "Why does this man speak thus? It is blasphemy! Who can forgive sins but God alone?" This is an action which only God can perform, and yet Jesus claims it as his own right. Jesus does not stand there and say, "I am God," nor does the Bible writer explicitly draw that conclusion. He lets *the action* speak for itself! The scribes are absolutely right! It *was* an axiom of Jewish thought that only God could perform or bestow forgiveness. By claiming this as his right, Jesus was putting himself equal to God! Indirectly, in terms of acts performed, the divinity of Jesus is being insisted upon.

Illustrations like this, using a description of action rather than a statement about Jesus' person, can be multiplied endlessly. Take, for example, the Sermon on the Mount, which begins in the fifth chapter of Matthew. One line, repeated over and over again, is: "You have heard that it was said to the men of old. . . . But I say to you . . ." What was said of old? Why, God's word was! Moses, standing on Mt. Sinai, delivered the word of God. But now Jesus, standing on another mount, speaks again and fulfills and replaces that ancient hallowed word: "But *I* say to you . . ." He puts his own word equal to and above the revealed word of God given through Moses and treasured through the centuries by the Jews as the ultimate revelation of the living God who had ripped them out of Pharaoh's furnace! Jesus nowhere says, as a Greek would, "I am of the same substance as the Father." Instead, the Bible writer, by showing Jesus in action, requiring the same obedience to his own word as had been given to God's word delivered through Moses, is insisting on the divinity of Jesus.

The same thing can be said about Jesus' humanity. He is shown as true man, but not shown as true man in Greek terms. Nowhere is the task of the later Greek theologian made easier by the insertion of phrases pointing to the stuff or essence or substance of Jesus (John 1:14, read in the light of John 1:1, comes about the closest, but even that verse has a complicated history behind it which we cannot go into here). Instead, the Bible writer points to the *acts* of Jesus. *Those* things prove his humanity. Jesus has to ask, "Who touched my garments?" (Mark 5:30). He does not seem to know! His knowledge is limited. He is a true human being circumscribed and limited by ordinary human insight. He flatly confesses that he does not know when the end of the world will arrive (Mark 13:32). He is wearied from a journey, must sit down at a well and rest and ask a passing woman for a refreshing drink of water (John 4:6–7); he weeps when a friend dies (John 11:35), and says he has no place to lay his head. He is tempted, tried to the core of his being, lured to the edge of evil (Matt. 4:1–11; Heb. 4:15; 5:2). This is not playacting, a stage drama translated into theological terms! The temptation scene is precisely a drama because, as far as the Bible writer is concerned, Jesus could have fallen! And the fact that he could have but did not is what makes the issue of the temptation scene so electrifyingly significant and important. He could have been overwhelmed, but he was not! He could have been overwhelmed because he was true man, not simply God incognito. True man, his actions showed it.

Yet he was true God too. The two stand, unresolved, contradictory, head-on opposites, and the two must be held together in tension. The person of Jesus will never be comprehended aright by denying or subordinating one side to the other.

But neither will the person of Jesus ever be rightly understood unless we see, with the Jewish Bible writer, that the really important thing about Jesus was not his person but his work—not so much who he was but what he was able to do.

HIS WORK

Personally, Tertullian was not a pleasant person. Born at Carthage in North Africa, sometime in the middle of the second century, he died there too, about A.D. 220. In between, for at least a time, he practiced law in Rome. Since he was a big Roman lawyer, his name is actually preserved on some Roman records or legal briefs. Not only legal, he was also legalistic in his thinking, at times even fanatic, and he died in disgrace, a member of the condemned Montanist sect. He was not a pleasant person. Puritanical and ascetic, extremely rigorous in his own ethical life, he was a harsh man, violent and vituperative in his denunciations of all those who did not agree with him. He had a forked tongue and an acid pen and a flaming sense of sarcasm with which he withered all who stood up against him. To win an argument he would stop at nothing, not even ridicule, insult, and calumny. But above all, he was a lawyer, and it was *that* factor which gave his thinking his characteristic mark.

Lawyers think in terms of *guilt,* in terms of crime and punishment, and that was the way this lawyer turned theologian interpreted the Christian faith. For him, sin was guilt and the answer was punishment. To explain the relationship of man to God, Tertullian used the legal analogy of the relationship of a property owner to his property. The property owner can do whatever he wants with his property. He can build a building on it, plant it in crops, or let it lie fallow. He can dig a swimming pool or a cesspool, build a city slum or grow exotic roses —the choice is his, he can do as he wills. It was in this unbending sense of sovereign or absolute majesty, of unbridled control, that he saw man under God. God was the owner; man was the obedient servant. But man did *not* obey—he rebelled, and that made him *guilty.* For Tertullian, there were two kinds of guilt. There was, first of all, *original* guilt. This was the taint you were born with, the natural evil inclination of a fallen human being: "Behold, I was brought forth in iniquity, and in sin did my mother conceive me" (Ps. 51:5). You were *born* sinful, guilty, and you had no control over that. But in the eyes of the law—and Tertullian was a lawyer—that over which you have no control is not laid against you. Christ's death on the cross, *that* paid the price of the Christian's original guilt. Once baptized, the slate was wiped clean. Christ's sacrifice was sufficient payment, and you were clean, born again, a guiltless person. Incidentally, this is why, once this idea of Tertullian's took root, men postponed their baptism as long as they could. When Constantine later became emperor and then a Christian, he put off his baptism until as late in life as possible. As long as the sacrament of baptism wiped the slate clean, it was best to wait as long as you could, make yourself spotless at the latest possible minute in life, better fitted to enter the halls of heaven.

But to Tertullian the second form of guilt was *actual* guilt, the guilt that accrued to you for evil acts you performed *after* you had been baptized. For those, *you* were responsible, *you*

had to pay the price. Jesus' suffering on the cross took care of
earlier or original guilt, but your suffering had to pay the price
of actual guilt. In the eyes of the law—and Tertullian was a
lawyer—some crimes are more serious than others; there are
degrees of wrongdoing, hence degrees of guilt. Even today we
speak of grand larceny and petty larceny, of big and little
thefts, with graduated scales of punishment. That idea Tertullian translated into religious terms. It was with him that the
idea of big and little sins—mortal and venial sins—first took
shape and form. The mortal sins were the ones that were so
bad they ruptured and destroyed the bond with Christ established in baptism. They cut you off entirely from God's grace,
and the punishment for them was eternal, forever in hell, forever separated from God. But the little ones, the venial sins,
the occasional lapses to which all are heir, could be atoned for
—*if* you paid the price, *if* you suffered, if *you* suffered, not
Jesus but you.

With that thought, all the seeds of later Catholic thought
were planted. They did not flower for centuries, but the seeds
were planted. The seeds of purgatory, of penance, of indulgences, of monasticism—all now were present in embryonic
form. A man could pay the price for his venial sins, balance the
scales of justice and make amends for his actual guilt, either in
this life or the next—but *somewhere*, in this life or the next, the
guilt had to be paid for. Thus monasticism was born, or at least
made theologically respectable. A man could punish himself,
here and now, and thus make things right. He could barricade
himself off from the world, purify his soul through self-imposed
suffering, and thus wipe out the guilt marked against his name.

This ascetic self-denying way of life had a double advantage.
On the one hand, by giving up society and its pleasures, by
suffering now, guilt was taken care of, burned off through
present suffering. On the other hand, by such self-denial the
actual acts of sin were cut down! How could a man be guilty
of gluttony or adultery, of lust or avarice, when he had given
up all things? Pride, maybe—that might mount up as a man
made marks on the wall of his cave, chalking up all his virtuous

acts of self-denial—but gluttony and adultery, at least *those* two were wiped out, earning no guilt, demanding no punishment. Monasticism, then, was one way, a double way, of dealing with guilt, of taking punishment right now and simultaneously cutting down on the number of temptations faced, thus making it possible to go straight to heaven after death, since the scales of justice were already balanced.

But for those who wanted it both ways, heaven later but a little of earth right now, another way was possible to deal with actual guilt. Here the seeds of purgatory, of penances and indulgences, were planted. If your bad acts earned demerits, your good acts could earn merits. The scales could be balanced in that way. Give alms, say prayers, perform meritorious works —all these things would go a long way in making the ledger come out right. And the church in its infinite mercy would one day help the belabored souls on this journey. To increase the number of good works available, certain religious rites, certain limited times of fasting and self-denial, came into practice. You did not have to be a monk *all* the time, just some of the time, such as at Lent. Fast then, perform a penance, a period of repentant self-denial, and this would help later on. Take a trip to the Holy Land and during Lent visit the spots where Jesus lived and suffered, renewing your devotion through such a pilgrimage. This would all help in balancing the scales, for this was a meritorious work.

But what if you could not go to the Holy Land? You had a broken leg? or a business to watch? or a blister? what then? Send someone else in your stead, maybe an uncle or a brother or a priest. Give money to the priest, and *he* would go for you and *you* would get credit for it. *Both* of you would get credit for it, you because you paid for the trip, the priest because he made the trip. So it came about (all this developed over a period of centuries, for Tertullian did not develop it all; he only planted the seeds, with his legalistic categories of thought, which allowed these ideas later to flower) that indulgences were brought into being. An indulgence was a concession offered by the church. Because you had performed such a good act, sent a priest to the Holy Land, spent that much money, you received so much grace. So much money spent, so much future suffering alleviated.

But even this was not always enough to balance the scales. Even with your good deeds, your periods of penance, and the indulgences bestowed, even with these you still had more demerits than merits, more guilt-earning acts than kindly deeds. Where was the difference to be paid? You were a Christian, baptized in Jesus' name. You had never committed a mortal sin, never broken the relationship. Obviously, therefore, you were not—could not be—lost. But the scales were not balanced, either. Where was the difference to be paid? In purgatory. That doctrine too finds its roots in Tertullian's view. A place of purgation, of cleansing, of being burned pure, where actual guilt melted away. Purgatory was an in-between place, neither heaven nor hell, but a midpoint in between. For a period of time, its length determined by your surplus of evil deeds, you had to undergo the pangs of this semi-hell. But when your time was fulfilled, you would go from purgatory to heaven, your actual guilt at last covered.

Now, as I said, Tertullian was eventually excommunicated, thrown out of the church, condemned as a heretic, because he joined the mad Montanists. Once he was condemned, his teachings were clouded over as well. Not only was the man tainted but his ideas too. Cyprian, another North African, learned to love what Tertullian had said, and even called Tertullian "master." But that was the point! He had to call him "master," could not even call him by his name, for the name of Tertullian was anathema, the name of a heretic. This is why what Tertullian said took so long to flourish and flower, not creeping back into respectable circles for centuries. But it *did* creep back! It crept back for this one fundamental reason: Tertullian wrote in Latin! He was born at a critical moment in the life of the church. The pendulum was swinging from East to West, from Greek to Roman. Latin was coming into its own and was soon to be the language of the church, as it was for centuries. Greek was dying out. A new vocabulary was being formed. Theological ideas had to be translated from one tongue into another. A new means of expression had to be hammered out—words invented, concepts formed, ideas created that were able to say in one language what had earlier been said in another. At that critical moment, Tertullian wrote in Latin. The Catholic Church could and did call Tertullian a heretic, but it inherited his language. It was he who shaped the framework of the later Latin-speaking Catholic Church. It was he who gave the church its Latin vocabulary, the first man ever to write theology in the Latin language. And that later Latin-speaking church forever bore the imprint of the lawyer's thought, and forever saw sin as *guilt* for which a price had to be paid.

Centuries rolled by, however, centuries in which the ideas of Tertullian, unformed and never welded into a system, filled the air. But finally there appeared a man named Anselm, who took this raw material of Tertullian's thought and fashioned it into a cohesive, comprehensive theological interpretation of the work of Christ. It was Anselm who first formulated the work of Christ into a complete theological picture. And for Anselm, sin was *guilt,* an objective bundle of blackness, the accrued staining residue resulting from man's evil acts—guilt that demanded a price.

Anselm spent the most productive part of his life in Britain as Archbishop of Canterbury, but he was not British. He was born in A.D. 1033 in Piedmont, a territory in the Alpine country in the Switzerland area of northern Italy. A church politician, a philosopher, and a theologian, Anselm wrote many things. Much of his life was spent in that maelstrom which later historians call the investiture struggle, the argument over whether or not the pope has the right to name a bishop in a foreign land or whether that right belongs to the local king. He also wrote the *Proslogion,* a document that makes all philosophers clap their hands because it proves the existence of God, the famous ontological argument.

The thing that concerns us here, however, is not his writings on church politics or philosophical issues, but rather his theological work *Cur Deus Homo,* roughly translated, "Why did God become man?" He is asking, and answering, the question, Why Jesus? What was the reason, the purpose, behind the incarnation, the coming of Jesus to earth?

The answer he gives begins where Tertullian began. God is sovereign, the ruler over all. He has absolute control over man, even as a property owner is sovereign over his estate. But man has not respected that sovereignty, man has rebelled, and thus rendered himself guilty. Man has robbed God of honor and thus he stands condemned. A price must be paid, restitution offered. But man cannot make that payment! He cannot, because even if man, a sinner, turned over a new leaf and resolved to rob God no more, what merit would there be in that? What bonus or offsetting merit has man gained? For me to be good *now* does not cover the wrong I did *then.* If, for the sake of argument, I could be perfect from here on out, all I have done is to have been a faithful servant, simply doing what is required of me. I have gained no new demerits, true, and in that sense my efforts have been worthwhile. But neither have I earned any merits that would cover over my wrongs of yesterday. Hence the dilemma. Man owes a price, but man is unable to pay that price! Only God can pay the price, but God does not owe it, man does! Hence the dilemma. Man is in debt and cannot pay. God can pay, but God is not in debt!

The answer? God must become man. He must enter into the human realm and pay the price man cannot offer up. *Cur Deus Homo?* So that the scales can be balanced and guilt covered over, satisfaction offered up for that objective bundle of guilt weighing on man.

That, in a nutshell, is the thrust of this famous formative work, *Cur Deus Homo.* Jesus volunteers to do what man cannot do. God's justice must be satisfied. God has been robbed, and honor demands that a price be paid. God cannot forgive by simple fiat, condoning sin, making out it never happened. To blink an eye at wrong is to identify with it. God cannot condone—that would be unjust, wrong. But he can atone, himself pay the price, himself satisfy the debt owed. And that is what

Jesus does. He becomes man in order to undergo our punishment, he pays our debt, balances the ledger, satisfies God's justice, makes it possible for man to return to fellowship with God. A weak illustration: today a father can pay a traffic ticket for a wayward son, reaching into his own wallet to pay the legal debt contracted by the boy. The illustration *is* weak. It breaks down, of course, in that while this can be done for traffic tickets, it cannot be done in felony cases. No one can, or should, perhaps, go to the gas chamber in place of another. But allowing for the weakness of the illustration, it *is* a good illustration, at least in the sense that it amply recognizes the legal aspect of Anselm's thought, and powerfully stresses the idea of one person's (here Jesus') paying the price owed by another.

That is Anselm's understanding of the work of Christ. He stresses the justice of God. And he stresses the vicarious suffering of Jesus. Jesus, on the cross, undergoes the punishment we ought to have borne. He makes satisfaction for us. This is what gives Anselm's theory its name. This theory of the atonement, of the work of Christ, is called to this day the "satisfaction," or the "penal," theory, Jesus being penalized or punished in our place, Jesus rendering up the satisfaction to God's justice that we are unable to make. The whole thing traces back to the basic conviction, first formed by Tertullian, that *sin is guilt*. This is one of the three ways in which *the work* of Jesus has been interpreted. *His person* is subordinate to, or determined by, the work he has to do. He has to be God, because only God can pay the debt, but he has to be man as well, for it is man who owes that debt.

But a reaction was bound to come. Anselm's God is cold and passionless, foreboding, devoid of compassion. It is God's *justice*, God's legal demands, that have to be satisfied. The picture is as warm and comforting as the wooden bench of a courtroom. Anselm himself seems to have sensed this sterile and stern barrenness. In one of his writings, in a passing but profound insight, he pens these words: "Why, Lord God, doth my soul not feel thee if it hath found thee?" There is this cold and chilling sense of man's standing not before a compassionate Father who kills the fatted calf when the wayward son repents and returns but, rather, the Shylock demanding his pound of flesh, ripping out his portion no matter who suffers, even his own Son, Jesus. If the idea of the love of God survives at all, it survives only in the Son and not in the Father. We end up splitting the Godhead, setting the sacrificing Son against the legal demands of the Father.

Why does God not just *forgive?* Why does he *punish* and forgive? Anselm had a profound insight: the holiness of God, his justice which establishes morality and righteousness. There *is* such a thing as right and wrong, all things are *not* relative, it *does* make a difference what you do, and how you behave causes suffering, either for yourself or for others about you, and that is the way it is. Anselm saw that there are moral principles ingrained in the very substance of the cosmos, and that when we do not obey those rules of the cosmos a price is exacted. Violate the rules, you wreak havoc and reap despair. If I jump off the Eiffel Tower, I do not break the law of gravity; it breaks me! That is the way it is. There are laws in this world, physical laws of gravity, that I have to respect or pay the consequences. There are moral laws as well, and if I go wenching and whoring about, I'll pay the price there too! That is what Anselm is saying. He has a profound insight: that man is a moral creature, created in such a way that the absolutes of a moral cosmos are woven into his very fiber, and that when man's freedom is abused, a price is demanded. Saying, "I'm sorry!" is not enough. Halfway down, after I have jumped off the Eiffel Tower, I cannot say, "Oops, a mistake!" and turn back and climb up again. What I have done remains an objective fact even after my subjective stupidity is past. Saying, "I'm sorry" is not enough—*somebody*, in this case me, is going to pay the price. I will have a broken head and a broken leg. But in the religious sense, Jesus paid the price. His side was punctured, his hands were pierced, his blood flowed. He paid the price, and justice was satisfied. A profound picture (but a cold one, for the warmth is not in God but in the Son who stepped into my place), the picture of a demanding God, dominated by justice alone, devoid of compassion, emerges. A reaction was bound to come. Even Anselm felt the chill of his own thought, "Why, Lord God, doth my soul not feel thee?" And that reaction came with Peter Abelard.

Abelard was a fascinating man. He had one of the most caustic, vitriolic tongues found anywhere in theology. Pugnacious, haughty, devastatingly sarcastic, he once reduced one of his teachers to academic blubber by writing that this man wished to light a fire to give off light but that all he did was make a lot of smoke! You just did not talk about your teacher that way—unless you were Abelard. A man who lived life to the gleaming hilt, he poured himself with passion and emotion into all that he did. He had an extremely high regard for himself which demanded, by the logic of an Abelard, of course, a correspondingly low evaluation of everyone else. He made a few enemies.

Born in France, in Brittany to be exact, in A.D. 1079, a generation or so after Anselm's death, he was at first a teacher of philosophy—and a good one. Students flocked to him, which, of course, did not make him any more popular with his enemies when *they* took attendance in *their* classrooms in front of empty benches, all the students having gone over to Abelard! But the big things of the world go on in theology, not philosophy, and so he eventually wandered over into the queen of the sciences, the study of theology—and he was a good teacher there too.

But then, always an emotional and passionate man, he fell in love with the beautiful Héloïse, a love so touching in its depth and tragic in its issue that Rousseau was one day to use the story as a model for his novel *La Nouvelle Héloïse*. Héloïse was the niece of one of Abelard's fellow teachers, Fulbert by name, and she and Abelard were married secretly. Not knowing of the marriage and enraged beyond reason when he heard that the two were sleeping together, Fulbert decided to teach the young intellectual whippet a lesson he would never forget. He had Abelard seized and castrated. Never again would he sleep with Héloïse.

I mention this event with Héloïse because, tragic though it is, it is a basic indication of the character of this man Abelard. He was sarcastic, yes, but even more, a romantic, a man of emotion, of passion, and in his theology as well as in his life with Héloïse, primacy is given to passion. There is a warmth of life, a certain emphasis on the vitality and centrality of love, which, denied him in his physical life, is spilled out in his later theological writings. From this point of view, he was poles apart from Anselm, from the cold mechanical and impersonal process of legal justice that characterized the "satisfaction," or "penal," theory of the atonement.

For Abelard, sin was not guilt, a cold objective bundle of accumulated stains. Instead, *sin was rebellion,* a living, subjective, passionate thing vibrant with life. It was evil life, passion poured out in the wrong direction, but still it was life, warm, vibrant, pulsating. It was life gone wrong, subjective life perverting what life ought to be, man wasting himself chasing after phantoms. For Abelard, sin was rebellion.

For Abelard, God was not a judge, a legal complex, a bundle of rules to be respected, and a dispenser of punishment when those rules were broken. For Abelard, God was a person, a living, moral feeling person who wept when his sons went away from home and who rushed out of the house hurling wide the doors when the prodigal reappeared on the horizon. When wandering man came back from the far country, God rushed out and killed the fatted calf and put a ring on the prodigal's finger, shoes on his feet, and held a party! There was no objective barrier of guilt standing in the way, only the subjective rebellion of the wanderer who had run away from home. Rebellion ended, all was back in order, fellowship reestablished. Simply to say, "I'm sorry" and come home was enough. God asked no more.

And what was the work of Jesus? To make us come home. To make us turn over a new leaf. To make us stop running and return. To renew us morally, make us change subjectively. And that is the name of the theory formulated by Abelard. It is called the "moral renewal" theory. Man repents, renews himself, undergoes a moral change.

Our problem is that we do not know—we do not *really* know—that God loves us, cares for us. We look at suffering and pain on every side, we have it dinned into our heads by Anselmic emphases on justice, that God is an avenging God, a bookkeeper at best, a tyrant at worst, punishing us when we fall, pounding us with pain when what we need is comfort and compassion. Why suffering? Why castration when you want to love a woman? Are these the acts of God? Manifestations of his justice? Is *that* the kind of God who lives in the caverns of the heavens above, One who would heap on us sorrow on top of our shame? Such a God is not worth knowing, Abelard would argue. The God *he* argued for was a forgiving God, who forgave *without* punishment. When I see that I am wrong and say that I am sorry, this is enough! When once I know that God *does* care, I will turn, renew myself morally, ending my days as a vagrant, and come home as a son.

But what makes me turn? What makes me come home? What *proves* to me that God loves me? Look at the cross! There is the answer! We take this Jesus and rip apart his arms, spreading them wide to nail him to a crossbar, and what does he do? Pontificate as a judge and promise punishment in purgatory? No! He spreads those arms even wider, and stretching out those agonized limbs he pronounces benediction and forgiveness, without threat: "Father, forgive them; for they know not what they do!" *That* is the work of Jesus! He reveals the *love* of God. He makes it clear, unmistakable, radically renewing, compulsively compelling. Who can resist so great a love that even as we turn on him he calls us blessed? When we are face to face with the loving Jesus, our hostility evaporates, our subjective rebellion disappears, and we repent. We come home. "Were you there when they crucified my Lord?" So sings Marian Anderson in her great spiritual, expressing a sentiment first formed by Abelard, centuries ago. If you *were* there, if you stand, symbolically, at the foot of the cross, hammer in hand, driving nails through the living hands and feet of Jesus, if you see that *he* died because of *your* rebellion and that *despite* this rebellion he loves you, then how can you continue to resist? Rebellion melts away even as the rising sun burns off the dew of a dampened evening. A new day is here, the Son of God's love is seen, we know that he cares, and life begins once more. Now we no longer live a life of obstinate perverse rejection, but we love because he first loved us.

This is Abelard. This is the second explanation of the work of Christ, the "moral renewal" theory. Man turns over a new leaf, responds to the love of God, and it all revolves around the idea of sin as *rebellion*.

There is a great and self-evident value in all that Abelard said. We see at once the intrinsic worth of his theory. It unfolds again and anew the vital provocative center of that ancient message which once electrified the world—God cares! The value is self-evident and enormous, and thus the dangers of the theory are often overlooked. It affirms the reality of God's love, but the insight of Anselm, and he did have an insight, is now in great danger. What of moral absolutes, what of inviolable laws? Is there really, beyond my own attitude, no right or wrong? Is there no objective standard against which I am measured and which, when I violate it, stands against me, condemning me? Is it true that simply saying, "I am sorry," is enough? What does this do to morality? More, is this true to life? *Does* the drunkard who squandered his life and ruined his liver get back the lost years and a new liver simply by turning over a new leaf? Or is it not instead true that the scar remains and a price is wrung out of us *even though* God loves us? Does this not, in the deepest sense, deny *all* morality, by indicating that it really does not make any difference what we do or how long we do it, as long as we repent in time? Is not that the opening of the door to the worst kind of anarchy—moral relativism?

These are not idle questions aimlessly asked. It is a matter of incontrovertible historical fact that those who followed after

Abelard were quick to seize on these very points. What Abelard was really saying, it seemed to many who took up his cause, was that it did not make so much difference *what* you did as *why* you did it! The *motive* was all that counted. When you had bad motives and ran away from God, all was lost. But when your motives were reformed and you were renewed, the past was forgotten and the future renewed. As long as your *thoughts* were right, your deeds were relatively unimportant, because you could no longer think in legalistic terms of this *wrong* deed earning punishment, and that *right* deed offsetting the wrong ones. Indeed, you could not think of deeds, only of motives, of attitudes. Did you love or did you hate and rebel? That and that alone was the question.

This point led directly and swiftly to one of the vilest blots on the history of the church. There were no longer any external rules, absolute commandments, arbitrary laws bearing punishment or exuding grace. All that counted was motive. The seeds of the Inquisition were thrust into the earth, later to bear bitter fruit. The Inquisitors honestly felt that by inflicting awesome tortures on heretics here they could make them repent and enter into a new and better life later. Their motive was good and their aim ideal—the salvation of souls. What could be more noble? But from their activities came a wake of battered bodies, beaten people, wracked and ruined lives, the vicious heritage that the end justified the means.

The pendulum swung, perhaps too far. Anselm had an insight, but by itself it was cold and sterile and sullen. Justice alone existed, but justice was not enough. Abelard had an insight: that God was not basically a judge but a lover. Love alone existed, but love was not enough. Both by themselves tell us something, a truth, but because it is truth sundered from countertruth, corrective insight, it becomes no truth.

Abelard and Anselm lived centuries ago and centuries ago formed two of the three ways in which the work of Jesus can be understood. The third point of view, or third theory of the atonement, was also shaped by a man whose name begins with A—Gustaf Aulén—but he did not live centuries ago, he lives

today. He is the Bishop of Lund, Sweden, the primate of the
Swedish Lutheran Church. In a thin but incisive little book
entitled *Christus Victor* the broad lines of this third view are
laid clear. You might as an immediate consequence therefore
conclude that, since Aulén is a man of our day, this is a modern
theory, the most recent on the scene.

However, the first and primary point that Aulén tries to
make is just the opposite, namely, that the view he presents
is not the latest on the scene but rather the oldest interpretation of the work of Christ known to the church. He tries to get
that idea across by naming this view the "classic" theory of
the atonement. Classic, it goes back to the golden days of the
church, when the church was beginning. This, he argues, is the
first view the church ever held, and the theories of Abelard
and Anselm are later interlopers on the field.

In essence the whole theory is wrapped up in the title of his
brief book *Christus Victor:* Christ the strong man, Jesus the
conqueror, the Lord triumphant, beating down every power
and foe that faces man. The emphasis is not on justice nor on
love but on *power*. Power over whom? Here, to answer this
and understand the answer, an effort of will must be made.
You have to lift yourself up out of your twentieth-century
thought categories and strive strenuously to put yourself back
into the shoes of the earliest church—learn to think as they
did, accept the realities they saw as realities, and go on from
there. The church of long ago believed in the reality of the
devil. The devil was no comic figure, as he is in modern days,
sporting a flashy new pair of red pajamas, a goatee, cute little
horns, and carrying around a toasting fork that spurts flames
out of the end with which he prods you in the bottom every
time you pinch your neighbor's wife or sneak a cigarette behind the barn. Satan is no quaint archaic figure out of the
Middle Ages whose prime goal is to inspire witches and make
cows cease giving milk.

Satan was, for the early church, an awesome reality, a cosmic
dimension of evil, the source of all suffering. The doctrine took
root in those tragic days, about a century and a half before

Jesus was born, when Antiochus Epiphanes, a mad Greek, was persecuting the Jews, battering them from pillar to post. Antiochus *was* mad. The name he had taken for himself, "Epiphanes," indicates that. The word means "the Shining One." He saw himself as the light of the world, the hope of all mankind. An heir of Alexander, he aspired as did Alexander, to spread Greek culture, Greek philosophy, across the face of the earth. What we often overlook about Alexander is that he not only conquered the world but also built libraries. Alexander marched not only with the soldier's sword but also with the librarian's card, and the city he built and named after himself, Alexandria, in Egypt, had the richest library the ancient world ever knew. Why? Because Alexander had a sense of destiny, a flaming vision, a driving purpose. And well he should have— he had a good teacher, Aristotle.

One day Aristotle was brewing tea (or whatever else men brewed in those days) and as the water pot boiled on the hearth, he watched the water vapor rise from the pot and condense. Eureka, that was it! A Greek, always looking for unchanging laws, scientific truths of unchanging nature, always a scientist, Aristotle saw something. He saw that water always acted that way. Heat it, you get vapor or steam; cool it, and you get condensation above. That was the way nature worked, that was an immutable law! Man, knowing that immutable law, could change the world, control his own destiny, make the deserts bloom! Nature did it now. The sun was the heat; water evaporated and went up. There in the heavens it cooled and made clouds and then rained. Nature did it. But now man knew the rules, *he* could do it! How? Well, that was a technical detail which would have to be worked out later (Big fires, maybe, who knows? *Something* could be worked out) but it *would* be worked out! Man could shape his environment, make rain, make the deserts bloom, change the history of the world, for geography is latent history. Man could alter his own destiny! Man the master of his ship, the captain of his fate. *That* was Hellenism! *That* was the gospel Alexander preached, the vision that drove him to the ends of the earth with the librarian's card! Even as he conquered the world of politics, so also man could conquer *every* world in which he walked. A glorious, affirmative, optimistic, thrilling evaluation of man as a giant! That was Alexander, and that was the heir of Alexander, Epiphanes the Shining One, the light of the world!

But how could he share this new light with the Jews? That was where Epiphanes lived and ruled, over the land of the Jews. Well, first of all, before one can plant, one has to plow— and plow he did. The old ways had to be suppressed and ripped up, Jewish religion destroyed, the way prepared for Greek optimism, an affirmation of man. And so Antiochus began his repressive work of plowing by proscribing the Books of the Law. No longer was Moses to be read. Further, the Temple was defiled. Antiochus herded swine into the Temple and had them butchered there on the altar, their spilled blood draining down over the holy place of Israel's religion. As everyone knows, the Jew to this day believes that the pig is an unclean animal, pork not to be eaten. Also, the Jew believed that life was in the blood. That was self-evident. If someone bleeds long enough, his life drains away and he dies. Life is in the blood. And the pig's blood was unclean. Yet that unclean blood oozed across the altar of Yahweh. The Temple was polluted, the abomination of desolation. But that was only the beginning, not the end. The law of Moses commanded circumcision for the male infant on the eighth day of life. No circumcision, said Epiphanes. If a child was circumcised, the priest who performed the ceremony was executed on the spot. The child was put to death immediately. The father of the dead child was slain, and the corpse of the babe was fastened around the neck of the still living mother and allowed to rot there, carrying away the mother in the putrefaction and stench of her own dead baby.

Out of that night of horror and hell came the doctrine of Satan. The Jew, the pious Jew, seeing suffering on every side, seeing that it was the one who remained loyal to the law who suffered most of all, came to the conclusion that the tragedies of the present hour were not, could not be, the work of God. How could God, who was just and loving, perform such atrocities? Suffering was out of all proportion to sin! Suffering was not a punishment for sin, for it was precisely those who did *not* sin, who tried to live under the laws of God delivered through Moses, who bore the brunt of that mad man's wrath. Thus was born the belief in Satan, the revolt of the heavenly council, the fall of the angels. The cosmos had gone berserk; the world was no longer under the immediate control of God. The devil had taken over. He who was formerly a servant in Old Testament thought became an enemy. It was he, not God, who was the source of all anguish. Suffering was not a judgment of God on the faithless, but an attack by Satan on the faithful. To be loyal to God in a world overrun by demonic forces opposed to God was to be subject to suffering of an awesome dimension. That is why Epiphanes prevailed! Because he was the servant of the devil himself, the devil who ruled this fallen, tragically enslaved planet.

This conviction, born in the days of Epiphanes as an attempt to explain the agonies of that day, is reflected from one end of the New Testament to the other. Revelation 12:7 explicitly refers to the "war [which] arose in heaven" speaking of this cosmic revolt, the fall of the angels, and then that passage goes on to insist that God cleared up the revolt upstairs, put down the rebellion in the high places, and threw Satan out. But where did he go? To the earth! Revelation 12:12, "Rejoice then, O heaven and you that dwell therein!" Certainly, *they* can rejoice! God's will *is* being done in heaven, the revolt overcome. *But*—"But woe to you, O earth and sea, for the devil has come down to you in great wrath, because he knows that his time is short!" That is the way Rev. 12:12 concludes. The havoc that Satan cannot hurl around the heavenly scene, having been driven out from there, he unloads on earth. That is why Antiochus could rule and exercise his malignant will, and that is why there is suffering, undeserved suffering, on every side.

I am not even going to argue here that this whole point of

view strikes modern man, technologically oriented and scientifically acclimated, as just a little bit absurd, perhaps. That is not really the point. The real point is that the earliest church believed such to be so! The Bible is studded with insistences that the true ruler of the present scene is not God but Satan. In Gal. 1:4, Paul speaks of the "present *evil* age" and in II Cor. 4:4, he tells *why* the present age is evil—because the "god of this world" is Satan. Ephesians 6:12 speaks the same way, calling the "*world rulers* of this present darkness . . . the spiritual hosts of wickedness in the heavenly places." The writer of I John 5:19 insists that the "whole world is in the power of the evil one," and twice the Gospel of John calls Satan the "ruler of this world" (John 12:31; 16:11).

The New Testament not only clearly insists that the devil rules this world, but it also goes on to insist emphatically and unambiguously that all the ills of this world are due to Satan, not to God. In Luke 13:16, Jesus stands confronted by a little old lady, bent over nearly double like a German pretzel, and he flatly says that for eighteen years *Satan* has bound that woman! Sickness is a work of the devil; that is the clear and unmistakable meaning of the passage, made even more clear and more unmistakable by the first six verses of that same thirteenth chapter of Luke where Jesus flatly denies that suffering is meted out as just retribution for sins committed. The New Testament also insists that Satan causes hunger as well as sickness. Jesus is alone in the wilderness for forty days and he is hungry. The first temptation is to turn the stones into bread and eat. In Rom. 8:35–39, Paul speaks of that cosmic army of evil spirits oppressing man and trying to separate him from the love of God, and right there, numbered among the prime weapons used by those fallen principalities and powers, is famine! Famine, persecution, the sword. And even with that the New Testament is not content. It goes on to insist that the greatest weapon of Satan is not sickness or hunger, but death! When you are hungry you can pray for a harvest, when you are sick you can look for surcease from sorrow, but when you are dead there is no hope. The chilling hand of the tomb stills all hope and speaks its inevitable final, "No!" Ask any parent who has ever stood over the crib of a dead child, dead before it ever lived, dead at the age of four or younger, and you know something of the awesome absurdity of death, denying all our hopes, and smashing all our dreams. And death, the New Testament insists, is the last great enemy, the final ultimate weapon of the evil one (I Cor. 15:26). Hebrews 2:14 emphatically insists that the devil is the cause of death: ". . . who has the power of death, that is, the devil."

So far, so negative. But, on the one hand, negative and dreary as the picture so far sounds, it is *not* a negative point of view. On the other hand, no matter how alien such views may seem to us today with our television sets and doses of penicillin, these views were *not* alien and bizarre to the earliest church. It is out of the fabric of this belief in the demonic that the powerful positive message of the earliest church was woven! This is the raw material of the *Christus Victor* motif, the emphasis on the *power* of God in Christ! Jesus promises that God's will *will* be done on earth as it is in heaven, God's Kingdom *will* come. The strong man has met his match and his master in Jesus of Nazareth, the divine Son of God. Satan causes hunger? Jesus feeds the multitudes! Satan causes sickness? Jesus makes the lame to walk, the blind to see, the broken, bent, and battered cripple to stand erect again! And Satan causes death? The whole verse of Heb. 2:14, quoted earlier only in part, insists that Jesus became a human being, took on our form, "partook of the same nature, that through death he might destroy him who has the power of death, that is, the devil."

For Abelard and Anselm, the cross of Jesus was the center and climax of all that Jesus did. It was in the cross of Jesus, said Anselm, that the justice of God was satisfied and a price paid to God. It was in the cross, said Abelard, that the last and ultimate expression of God's love was revealed, ripping man away from his old rebellious ways. But for the "classic" view, the cross is no end, only a means. It is the doorway through which Christ enters in order to storm the greatest weapon, death itself. He dies that he might overcome death! The resurrection, not the death, is his climactic great work! Here is where the victory is won! Even as he overcame hunger and sickness, so also now he shows with the empty tomb and the empty cross that here too he is stronger! *That,* says Aulén, is the original essence of the first Christian proclamation! It stresses primarily not the justice, not the love, of God, but the power of God. It begins on the assumption that sin is not rebellion or guilt but *bondage.* Man is enslaved, overwhelmed by this demonic foe he cannot resist, his whole life perverted and twisted, battered from within, beaten from without, his whole life wrapped up in shallows and miseries. The original exhuberant Christian proclamation, then, was not a plea for repentance, nor the pronouncement of a legal verdict of "not guilty." It was instead a shout of victory. What man could not do because he was a slave of Satan, God in Jesus had done!

There is much evidence that Aulén can muster, both out of the Bible and out of the writings of the later church fathers, to prove his contention that this was the primal or original interpretation of the work of Christ. Paul, for example, flatly and unqualifiedly insists, not once but twice, that the whole meaning and worth of Christianity is bound up with the reality of the resurrection: "If Christ has not been raised, then our preaching is in vain and your faith is in vain. . . . If Christ has not been raised, your faith is futile and you are still in your sins. . . . We are of all men most to be pitied" (I Cor. 15:14, 17–18). But he goes on to insist dramatically just a few verses later that "in fact Christ *has been raised* from the dead."

It is perhaps no accident that the earliest sermons of the church, as they are recalled in the book of The Acts, tell of the life and deeds and death of Jesus in a rather lackluster, unemotional way, but when those early preachers come to the resurrection, you can almost hear them suck in their breath and pound on the table, shouting out, of the resurrection, "Of this we are witnesses!" (see, for example, Acts 2:32; 3:15; 4:2; 5:32; *et al.*). It is also probably no accident that the earliest church chose as its day of worship, not the Sabbath, honored in Jewish tradition, nor Friday, hallowed by the death of Jesus, but instead, Sunday, the first day of the week, for this was the day that Jesus rose from the dead, conquering death. Each weekly worship was in effect a little Easter, a proclamation of Jesus' power over sin, death, and the devil. The church could get along for three centuries (down to the time of Constantine) without a Christmas, without a fixed day to celebrate Jesus' birth, but from the very beginning Easter was a reality, a necessity, the burning vibrant center of all that the church believed—that Jesus was stronger than death. Christ the conqueror had prevailed.

This, then, Aulén argues, is the first and fundamental way in which the work of Christ was originally understood and expounded. The emphasis is on the power of God. And it all traces back to the conviction that sin is *bondage*, that man is enslaved and helpless, open to the interference of the devil, who is working wrack and ruin across all of man's existence.

This is a profound insight, a valuable one, a comforting one. Hope is held high. There is the thrilling announcement that where man is unable, God is able, that whatever force or foe overwhelms man, God in Christ is stronger. The juxtaposition of the events of Mark, ch. 4, and Mark, ch. 5, serve as summary of the whole point of view. In Mark, ch. 4, Jesus stills the storm. In Mark, ch. 5, Jesus casts out the legion of demons besieging the poor afflicted. From wherever tyranny comes, from whatever foe man flees, Christ is the answer, the One giving liberation. When nature rages and the storms of the sea threaten to destroy us, when attacks come from the outside, Christ is stronger. When we are besieged from within by a legion of demons, no matter how we name them in the language of psychology, there Christ is stronger. Wherever the foe, inside or outside, Christ is the One who holds out hope and brings us victory. It is a profound insight, a valuable one.

But, valuable as it is, such a view cannot stand alone. In the first place, such a view—arguing that God is on our side, defeating the foe, insisting that God is not the source of suffering but rather the answer to it—while theologically satisfying, is philosophically naïve. It does not answer any of the problems it raises. For example, it says that suffering comes not from God but from Satan. But who created Satan, and why is his continued perverse activity tolerated rather than ended? The attempt to lift from God the opprobrium of making *him* responsible for suffering and sin ultimately fails. All that such a view does is to push the problem back one step, putting it in the heavens rather than on earth. Now it becomes easy to explain man's dilemma, the human predicament, for now one can look at sinful fallen man and say he is in bondage, that it is Satan who pushes him into sin. Man is not responsible for his actions, for sin is bondage. Well, all right, but who pushed *Satan* into sin? The problem of the origin of evil remains and still must be explained. Furthermore, this view has serious drawbacks in other areas as well. What does the *Christus Victor* view do to human responsibility? It may create hope, but certainly it also shatters or at least erodes any sense of personal accountability, destroying any desire or even any necessity to try to do better. It is all too easy simply to dismiss one's minor peccadilloes and major misdemeanors by pleading not guilty, not my fault, I am in bondage, and Satan pushed me. The essence of being a human being, the element of personal accountability, is denied.

What I am saying, then, is that each of these three major ways of looking at the work of Christ—Anselm's "satisfaction" theory, Abelard's "moral renewal" theory, and Aulén's *Christus Victor* or "classic" theory—has an insight, a valuable comprehension of the work of Christ, but each of them alone is insufficient. It is only when all three are taken together, combined and held in tension, that the full picture of Christ's work, of man's nature, of God's being, and of the nature of sin, falls into focus. Each of the three views tell us something, but only when all three are taken together. Look how, when all three views are held, the rounded robust picture emerges.

If you let all the implications of each area of the chart trickle into your cranium, you will see that every emphasis ever made within the church is included in it. When all three theories of

Formulator of Theory	Name of Theory	Nature of Sin	Nature of Man	Work of Christ	Place of Work	Nature of God Stressed	Nature of Jesus Stressed
Abelard	Moral Renewal	Rebellion	Responsible	Changing man's attitude — Producing repentance	Cross	Love	Human Model or Exemplar
Anselm	Satisfaction or Penal Theory	Guilt	Responsible	Changing God's attitude — Offering forgiveness	Cross	Justice	Human Atoner
Aulén	Classic or Christus Victor Theory	Bondage	Helpless	Changing Satan's role — Bestowing salvation	Resurrection	Power	Divine Redeemer or Liberator

the atonement are allowed to stand together, not as contradictory but as complementary, then the fullness of the Christian proclamation stands out in all its paradoxical, dialectical glory. Look at the chart again.

In our first chapter, we saw that sin could be defined in one of three different ways: as rebellion, as guilt, or as bondage. Or it could be seen in two different ways, an act or a condition. All are valid. All are recognized here. In Chapter Two we saw that the whole truth of man is not known until we say, holding opposites together in tension, that he is two things—responsible and self-determining, on one hand, and, on the other, often overwhelmed and in bondage. Both views of man show up on the chart.

Christ's work in the New Testament is described under a variety of headings as producing repentance, as offering forgiveness, as bestowing salvation. These are not synonyms and are not to be taken as such. They are separate, different concepts pointing to different views of sin. Jesus does all three. He demands—and his cross produces—repentance, making men turn around. The very verb "to repent" is a Greek verb of motion, meaning "to turn around," "to go back the other way." Man is going one way, running from God, and, like the prodigal son, he comes to his senses and goes home, rebellion ended, the cross having produced moral renewal.

The cross of Jesus provides forgiveness as well as produces repentance. Saying, "I'm sorry" is not enough. The stain, the guilt, must be washed away, and out of that insight comes the old gospel hymn "Are you washed in the blood of the Lamb?" The Gospel of John in its first chapter twice calls Jesus "the Lamb of God, who takes away the sin of the world." It is in the death of Jesus that man's guilt is covered, making him clean.

For Paul, the key word in his vocabulary is neither "repentance" nor "reconciliation" nor "forgiveness." It is salvation. To be saved is not the same thing as to repent or to be forgiven. It is another way of understanding the work of Christ, based on a different understanding of sin, sin as bondage, bondage to the devil from whom Christ in his resurrection power sets us free.

One can say the same thing in different terms, speaking of how Christ's work changes man's attitude, making him set aside his subjective rebellion. Or one can speak of how it changes God's attitude, satisfying his holiness, allowing him to see us anew as cleansed creatures, wiping away our objective guilt which remains even after we have repented. Or one can speak of how Christ's work alters our status, our condition, ripping us out of Satan's hands and uniting us to God, liberating us. Each of these motifs is incomplete in itself, preserving only partial truth, only a smaller part of the larger whole. The first two theories stress the cross and minimize or ignore the resurrection.

It is in the cross that we see the selflessness of Jesus, producing a selflessness in us as we seek to have in us the mind of Christ. The resurrection adds nothing. It is in the cross that forgiveness is made possible. There is no need for the resurrection, for which of the Old Testament sacrifices for guilt demanded the return to life of the victim in order to make the sacrifice efficacious? The emphasis is solely on the cross, and no resurrection is needed to complete it. In both of the first two views, then, the resurrection is irrelevant, it adds nothing. But in the third view, it is the cross that loses value as an end in itself. It is but a means, a doorway to victory. The heart of Christ's work is not dying but rising. It is the resurrection, the defeat of death, which is the last great enemy, that is the heart of Christ's work.

Each of these views is true, but by itself incomplete. The cross *is* important, but by itself incomplete. The resurrection *is* important, but the cross is not to be dismissed as merely a means to an end. It is only when all three theories stand side by side, not as options or competitive alternatives but rather as complementary additions one to the other, that the whole comprehension of Christ's work, of man's nature, and of the nature of sin, emerges.

God *is* love, justice, and power—not one of the three but

all three. He is concerned (love) and able to express that concern (power). But he is also just and holy, and expresses that concern in such a way that sin is not condoned but atoned. The work of Christ alters and makes new every attitude and area of man, changing man's own attitude, altering God's attitude, and transforming man's world. Jesus is held up in one instance as a model or exemplar, a human example to follow, and thus sense is made of those many Biblical imperatives which command and exhort man to set aside the old Adam and to have the mind of Christ. But Jesus is also held up as the divine redeemer, accomplishing what man cannot accomplish by himself.

All three of these theories or motifs are valid. Bible verse after Bible verse could be produced to support each of these affirmations on every square of our chart. That the squares conflict with one another does not mean that we are to choose one motif at the expense of the others. A further truth is that in actual Christian life all three of these theories do, in fact, stand together. In life they flow together, fuse, merge, mingle. They can be separated on a chart for teaching purposes but in life they are one. As a matter of fact, these things are so much one in life that often terms such as "reconciliation," "forgiveness," and "salvation" are used interchangeably, as if they were synonyms.

But precisely that is the problem. On the one hand, they are *not* synonyms. They speak of the *same* work of Christ, but they speak of it from different perspectives. On the other hand, since we do use these terms interchangeably, we sometimes fail to recognize that we are in actual fact confining and limiting ourselves to one section on the chart, one theory of the work of Christ, even though we use the language of all three sections, all three theories. We are basically Greek in our thinking. We look for order, we want logic to prevail, we try to harmonize opposites instead of allowing them to stand in tension. Thus, while we pay homage to all three aspects of Christ's work as prophet, priest, and king, while we use the language of all three theories, what happens is that we really lean primarily on one theory, and the other two become subordinate, if not flatly ignored. This is true not only of individuals but also of entire denominations.

For example, there simply can be no serious doubt of the fact that the *primary* (notice well, not the exclusive but the primary) emphasis of the Roman Catholic branch of Christianity is on sin as guilt. It is the Anselmic "satisfaction" or "penal" theory that is the determinative way for the broad lines of Roman Catholic theological thought. The symbol of the Catholic Church, seen at the head of the altar, is the crucifix: Jesus on the cross, suffering. That is the basic emphasis, the suffering Jesus, paying the price for our guilt, making atonement. Think of all the Catholic art that has come forward during the past centuries. The emphasis is always the same: it is the "satisfaction" or "penal" theory in paint. The crown of thorns plunged cruelly into the head, the *sacré coeur* motif where the chest is bared and the rib cage opened so that we can see the beating sacred heart breaking in pain on our behalf. Always, behind it all, is the basic conviction that sin is guilt and a price must be paid. This is seen not only in art, but even more in Catholic theology and liturgy. The whole sacrament of the Mass has emerged against the backdrop of sin as guilt and Tertullian's early understanding, worked out in Anselm, of original guilt and actual guilt. On the cross, suffering then, Jesus paid the price of our original guilt, and in baptism we receive the benefits of that suffering, our original guilt covered. But what of actual guilt, which is contracted *after* baptism? For that, Jesus suffers once more, every time Mass is said.

Basic to Catholic thought is the conviction that when the priest holds high the Host before the altar, Jesus once more is crucified, once more slain in a bloodless death making new satisfaction for actual guilt. Again, you see the emphasis is on the suffering Christ, because the emphasis is on sin as guilt for which a price is owed. Life as a ledger, sin as a debt, venial and mortal sins with lesser and greater punishments—all the ideas we saw in Tertullian and Anselm—remain. A saint, in Roman Catholic thought, is one whose good deeds outweigh his bad acts—his merits are of greater weight than his errors or wrong deeds. Such a one goes straight to heaven. But for the others, unable or unwilling to make such an effort, for those who have done more wrong than right, there is purgatory before heaven, the place where excess guilt is burned away. To lessen the years in purgatory and the hours of pain the church makes available, now as long ago, dispensations, indulgences, and penances. The whole structure of Catholic thought—its emphasis on purgatory, the concept of sainthood, the understanding of the Mass, the view of venial and mortal sins, the endorsement of penance and the belief in indulgences—the whole structure can be traced back to the basic conviction of Anselm that sin is guilt.

This is *not* to say that the other motifs and insights are absent. Sin is also seen as rebellion, and Catholic teaching includes not only Mass, penance, and purgatory, but exhortation as well. There is always the plea for personal renewal, for greater effort. There is an emphasis on the devil, on the reality of Satanic power, carrying with it the conviction that man is often not so much responsible as overwhelmed, a slave of powers he cannot resist. These other motifs are not absent, but neither are they emphasized, or central, or formative in nature.

The same can be said, from an opposite direction, for our Baptist brethren, for that wing of the church which we call Pentecostal, which includes many such names as Methodist along with Baptist and Pentecostal. They too have a belief in all three views of sin—rebellion, guilt, and bondage. They too have an emphasis, a central concept, to which the other two views are subordinate. For them, however, the central concept is not sin as guilt but rather sin as rebellion. That is why the Baptists, for example, have always been characterized by revival meetings, altar calls, pleas for repentance, demands for personal renewal and commitment. Sin is rebellion, and man is accountable. Of him an effort of will is demanded. "Give yourself to Jesus! Cease running from him and turn and come to him" is the cry. There is no elaborate structure of penance and purgatory, no stress on the sacraments as means of receiving grace to offset guilt.

One of the curious anomalies of current Christendom is the fact that the Baptists, the only Christian sect to take its name from one of the sacraments, does not believe that baptism is a sacrament, a work of God valid in itself! The name Baptist is in fact a shortened form of the longer name, Anabaptist. Baptism, in such a group, is not seen as an act of God dealing with original guilt. It is not an act of God at all. Rather, it is an outward sign of man's own inner act, a visible sign, made manifest through symbolic washing with water, that man has cleansed himself internally, religiously. Man has set aside his rebellion and replaced it with obedience. He has repented and been reconciled. No need is felt for an elaborate understanding of the Mass, of the Lord's Supper, as a source of satisfaction for sin as guilt, for sin is not seen as guilt but rather as rebellion—a rebellion for which there is but one answer, personal decision.

It is no accident of current theological history that the greatest name in this wing of the Christian proclamation—Billy Graham—has entitled his well-known program "The Hour of Decision" rather than, for example, "The Emphasis on Satisfaction." Man must decide. He must turn around, return home. He must come to the altar, make his stand for Christ, respond to the plea for repentance. There is no crucifix, no cruel crown of thorns, no *sacré coeur* motif. Or when there is an emphasis on the suffering of Jesus, it is developed in an entirely different way, a way that silhouettes and magnifies the great love of Christ, pleading with us to return, instead of stressing the vicarious satisfaction offered up by Christ to God in our stead. Again, this is not to say that sin as guilt or sin as bondage are not present. They are present. A good Baptist or Methodist or Pentecostal preacher has no hesitation in insisting that in Christ there is forgiveness, or that the devil is a real and malingering evil leading us astray. But while these motifs are present, they are woven into the fabric of a theology that sees sins basically as rebellion. They are background colors, secondary emphases always subordinated to one central and basic conviction that sin is rebellion.

And what of sin as bondage? In what denomination is that

motif preserved? A moment's reflection on the ground already covered makes that immediately clear. I have said that the *Christus Victor* or "classic" theory was vigorously argued for by Gustaf Aulén. I have also mentioned that he is the primate of the Swedish church, head of the Swedish *Lutheran* Church. It is in the main-line Protestant denominations such as those of Lutheranism or Calvinism that the stress on sin as slavery lies at the center of thought. It is the Lutheran who confesses every Sunday morning in the liturgy of his church, "We poor sinners confess unto thee that we are *by nature* sinful and unclean." It is the Lutheran who teaches his youngsters to memorize in catechetical training, as an explanation of the third article of the Apostle's Creed, "I believe that *I cannot by my own reason or strength* believe in Jesus." And it was Luther himself who not only threw an ink bottle at the devil but also went on to pick up the ink bottle and pen those words against Erasmus, the humanist, in his most famous work, *The Bondage of the Will*, that man is a beast of burden made to be ridden and is not even able to choose his own rider! That is why, historically, there have been no altar calls or revival meetings in the Lutheran Church, and no emphasis on the Mass or the suffering Christ on the cross, either. Sin is not seen essentially as rebellion, for which repentance is required, nor as guilt, for which a price must be paid, but as bondage, as Satanic power holding man helpless. That is why there stands at the head of every Lutheran church, not a crucifix commemorating the death of Christ, but rather an *empty* cross stressing the *power* of Christ, the *risen* Lord, the triumphant One doing in his might what man in his weakness is unable to do. That is why Luther was able to summarize the whole work of Christ in his one famous and cryptic line: Jesus has come to conquer sin, death, and the devil.

The major thrust of the Lutheran Church has always been the idea of God as power. Every Reformation Day, October 31, on pain of excommunication if you are off-key, the Lutheran has to sing "A Mighty Fortress Is Our God!" Read well the lines of the different stanzas of that hymn and you will see in capsule form the heart of Lutheran teaching. In stanza one, the hymn concludes by insisting that there is a mighty one who has no equal on earth. Who is that mighty one without an equal? Never sing the first stanza only, because in it that mighty one is not God but Satan who rules the world! *He* is the all-powerful one before whom we are helpless. But the hymn goes on to insist in the stanzas which follow that the Man of God's own choosing, Jesus Christ, has come forth and with a word shall overthrow Satan! Satan is strong, but Christ is stronger! *That* is historical Lutheranism. As a matter of fact, if time and space permitted, it could be successfully argued that the whole Lutheran Reformation was precipitated by the conviction of Luther that sin is not an act but a condition, not overt rebellion but bondage, Satanic servitude.

Tetzel and the church of his day insisted that sin was an act or a consequence of that act, rebellion producing guilt. To deal with the guilt, good actions were demanded, good actions that could be supplemented by penances and the purchase of indulgences. Luther railed against this because he was convinced that sin was basically entirely other. It was a condition, and a condition can be offset only by a new condition, not by good acts. That is why Luther insisted that man was saved, not by faith plus works, but by faith alone, a new condition created by God. Man had not created it, because he was a beast of burden made to be ridden and unable to choose his rider. He could not create a new condition by his own reason or strength. It could be created only by God—"God Alone." That was one of the great slogans or battle cries of the Reformation. So also was "Faith Alone." That was a synonym for the first phrase, not an addition to it. God alone created faith; it is a gift to helpless man, not a creation of man's will, a product of his repentance. The third of the three great Reformation slogans, "The Word Alone," grows out of the same interlocking set of ideas.

Luther insisted that sin was a condition, not an act. It was a condition with which or in which man was born, a condition which produced acts of sin. The individual acts of sin were not so much acts of sin as they were consequences of sin, or symptoms of that sinful condition. The individual acts of sin were like the spots you get when you have the measles. The spots are not the disease itself but the product of the disease. You do not cure the measles by painting over the spots; you do not cure sin by dealing with the symptoms, trying to offset the wrong acts by performing good acts. Sin is a condition of bondage into which you are born. Man is born with concupiscence, that is, with a tendency to perform wrong deeds, and *that concupiscence itself* is sin. Whether or not the condition ever actually breaks out into overt evil acts was, for Luther, an idle academic question. Of course it always did break out in such specific acts, but even if it did not, man would *still* be a sinner, for he was in that condition, that inner sickness of servitude. He had the measles even if you couldn't see the spots. To bolster this conviction, Luther, a New Testament scholar, a Pauline scholar, pointed to those places in Rom., chs. 6 and 7, where Paul actually speaks of sin as an invading force that has taken possession of him against his will. "The good which I would I do not. The evil which I would not, that I do. I can will what is right but I cannot do it. It is no longer I that do it but the sin which dwells within me." (Free translation of some of the lines of Rom. 7:15–20.)

It is an amazing thing that Luther's Catholic opposition saw far more clearly than did Luther's own followers what Luther was saying. In the Council of Trent, in those counter-Reformation struggles when the Catholic Church formulated anew its own convictions in opposition to the new threat of Lutheranism, the Catholic teachers saw exactly what Luther was saying. They went back and pored over the passages to which Luther had pointed in Paul, and they agreed that, yes, Paul had indeed called the condition itself sin, and had not limited the term "sin" to mean only the results of that condition. But, the Catholic Church went on, at this point Paul was wrong! The mother church had never so understood concupiscence to be sin but, rather, only *tending* toward sin. In the writings coming out of the Fifth Session of the Council of Trent, held June 17, 1546, in the Decree Concerning Original Sin, we read these words: "This concupiscence, which the apostle sometimes calls sin [and here reference is made specifically to Rom. 6:12 and 7:8] the holy Synod declares that the Catholic Church has never understood it to be called sin, as being truly and properly sin in those *born again,* but because it is of sin, and inclines to sin."

The Catholic exegetes looked at the same passages in Paul that Luther argued for, and there was no difference in their understanding of what Paul said and meant. Yes, they agreed, Paul does indeed agree that sin is a condition; he calls the condition of concupiscence itself sin. But Paul was wrong! The mother church does not see it that way! And it was from this that the third cry of the Reformation was born, "The Word Alone." When Catholic council or pope disagrees with the Scriptures, church tradition and interpretation is to be rejected and the Christian must take his stand on the clear meaning of the Word alone!

That the stress on sin as bondage is the primary historical emphasis of the Calvinistic branch of Christianity is, if anything, more clearly seen than in the Lutheran stream of tradition. It is only on this ground that Calvin's doctrine of double predestination could take root and flower. Man was helpless, enslaved. Only an act of God and an act of God alone could set man free from his servitude. Thus it followed that those who were saved were saved by divine decree alone, and those who were lost were lost through arbitrary divine decision alone. Calvin's predestination, the core of his thought, is but Luther's conviction carried forward to an extreme. Indeed, if there is any difference between the two men's thought at this point, this difference can be traced back to the fact that Luther was a New Testament scholar whereas Calvin was an Old Testament one. In the Old Testament the emphasis is on the sovereign omnipotence of God, a God of anger and wrath.

It is this stress on the arbitrary sovereignty of God which led to the sometimes extreme views of predestination argued for in the harsher Calvinistic circles. Man is saved or damned through no efforts or attitudes of his own but solely by virtue of the mysterious decrees of God. Luther was spared this excess because he was a New Testament scholar. He stressed the condescension of God, the compassionate intervention of Jesus on the cross. It was this love of God, and not Old Testament arbitrary wrath, which colored his thought. Luther too held a doctrine of predestination, but it was not a doctrine of arbitrary selectivity. Rather, it was a doctrine of comfort, the comforting assurance to the troubled believer that God was on his side, doing for him what he could not do for himself. Luther was neither logical nor consistent. He contented himself with saying solely that man was saved because of God's grace. He had a single doctrine of predestination. God is on man's side through Christ. But Calvin, more scholarly, more logically consistent, went on to posit the other side. If one is saved by God alone, then one is likewise damned by God alone. He had a double doctrine of predestination, one for the saved and another for the damned. Which of these men was right, if either, is not the point under discussion here. All that I am trying to show is that both of them worked within the categories of the "classic" theory: they both saw sin as being essentially bondage, man as helpless.

Again, this is not meant to deny that woven through Lutheranism or through Calvinistic thought there is an emphasis on sin as rebellion and sin as guilt as well. Those motifs are present, and a Lutheran as well as a Baptist or a Methodist can speak of personal decision, and a Calvinist as well as a Catholic can speak of forgiveness of guilt. Although those motifs are present, they are not formative and determinative for the mainstream of this current of Protestant thought. The empty cross, the risen Lord, the insistence that God is a Mighty Fortress— all these things make dramatically clear that the basic view is that of sin as bondage.

What I am saying, in effect, is that each of these three great denominational emphases—Catholic and Baptist and Lutheran —is correct, preserving one of the essential thrusts of Christian teaching. Each of them preserves and emphasizes a motif present in but not stressed by the others. Each of them has something to contribute and each preserves a truth, but a truth that must stand corrected by and complemented by the other truths. Any one of these motifs taken in isolation is no longer truth but heresy, for that is what heresy is. The word "heresy" itself, which has come to mean "false teaching," comes from a root word that does not mean error at all. It means "truth," but it is truth taken up and developed in isolation from other truths! Any one of these emphases taken exclusively without complement from the others is wrong, and perverts rather than proclaims Christian truth.

The Baptist, taken alone, with his basic thrust on man as responsible and called to account, can end up not with Christianity but with baptized humanism. We can so stress what *man* must do and how *man* must repent and come forward to the altar that we can squeeze God out of it entirely, reducing all to an effort of our own will, with God simply standing at the end of the process as a goal, or in the middle of the process as a cheerleader urging us on to greater efforts. But, on the other side, the Lutheran emphasis on sin as bondage and man as a slave, taken in isolation, is equally dangerous. What can happen is that the whole Christian structure can degenerate into a mechanical, magical, arbitrary process in which God capriciously saves one and rejects the other. Christianity can become an amusing celestial chess game where men, helpless men, are shuffled about like pawns on a board, devoid of all responsibility and calling.

The Bible speaks with *two* tongues. It stresses the divine sovereignty and, paradoxically, human responsibility. When we stress or isolate only one and lose the other, it is not that we have half the truth, but rather that we have no truth. These two different emphases must be held together, these different denominations need each other, for it appears that no one human head, no human denomination, by itself, is able to do full justice to the full, rich, varied emphases of the Christian faith. We need the Baptist emphasis on repentance, the Catholic insight that saying "I'm sorry" is not enough, the Lutheran emphasis on man's limits. These denominations need one another. Each by itself is a monotone. It is only when all three motifs or emphases are blended together that the full rich concert of God's harmony is heard, and we see the entire picture: sin is rebellion, guilt, and bondage; God is love, justice, and power; the resurrection and the cross are both important; man is both helpless and responsible; Jesus is both human model and divine redeemer.

This is both the promise and the threat of the modern ecumenical movement. We live in a day and age when, for the first time in many centuries, Christians of different persuasions are at last able to come together and fellowship as brothers in the faith. The pressures of an outside secular world, in which the Christians find themselves suddenly a minority, are doing wonderful things for the church. Now, instead of Catholic excommunicating Protestant, instead of Lutheran denouncing the pope as antichrist, we have these varying versions of Christianity able to come together and talk. In that is the promise. For the first time in centuries we stand in the anteroom of the concert hall, ready perhaps to go in and hear the full symphony of God's goodness as each denomination makes its own peculiar contribution.

The promise is great, but the threat is also great. The one great fear that stands before us is the potential or lurking danger that in this quest for greater brotherhood, we may end up seeking the lowest common denominator. Our drive to come together may dissipate in us, stressing only that which we share and have in common, causing us to minimize or ignore our differences. If we succeed in that search for unanimity, our very success will be our greatest disaster. A virtue can be a vice. If the quest for unity leads to uniformity, the very diversity that allows the fullness of the Christian faith to stand forth in all its varied splendors will be lost. The ecumenical movement can be the most disastrous thing ever to hit the church, far more destructive than the convulsion of the Reformation itself ever was, for it can lead to a soft-pedaling of differences, a loss of divergent insights, the disappearance of the many paradoxical affirmations of the different denominations. A good

Baptist ecumenicist is a good ecumenicist only when he is a good Baptist, and the same is true of all the others. It is only when each individual heritage is reaffirmed and articulated anew, rather than subordinated to some lowest common denominator upon which all can agree, that the ecumenical movement will bear the full fruit that lies embryonic in its womb. The different denominations need each other, but they need each other as *different* denominations.

Chapter Four

THE CHURCH

IN the preceding chapter we saw that there are three ways of understanding the work of Christ, based on the three different views of sin: sin as rebellion, as guilt, and as bondage. These three different theories of the work of Christ represent the major emphases of the Pentecostal groups, the Catholic Church, and the Lutheran-Calvinistic groups respectively. These varying emphases have extraordinary and far-reaching implications for the understanding of the sacraments, the nature of the church, the role of the Holy Spirit, and the nature of faith which is held by these different denominations. We begin with the views of the Catholic Church and with a review and an enlargement of some of the material given in the last chapter, moving on from there to new material.

The Catholic Church puts its major thrust on the idea of sin as guilt and Christ as atoner. This determines the way in which the sacraments are seen. For example, baptism takes care of original guilt, wiping out the primeval bent of man's inherited nature. The death of Christ pays the price for man's fallen nature, and the benefits of that death are made available to the individual in baptism. Once he is baptized, that original guilt is dealt with, taken care of, no longer charged against his account. The emphasis, then, is double—the sacrament is *objective* and it *looks backward.*

"Objective" means that the act of baptism is valid in itself. It does not depend for its efficacy or effectiveness upon the subjective faith of the person being baptized. The stress is on the ceremony as an act of God, not a self-consecration of man. The ceremony actually accomplishes something in its own right, independently of any feelings or response in man. It is an objective act that wipes out original guilt, and, since the act is objective, it can be performed on infants, on those too young to have any personal response of faith. The sacrament looks backward in that the rite is not understood so much as preparation for a proper future life, giving man power and purpose to live rightly from that moment on, but, rather, its stress is on wiping the past slate clean, doing away with that original guilt.

Once an individual is baptized, man's accountability swings into view. From the moment of baptism onward, the individual is responsible for actual guilt, for dealing with the demerits accrued by wrong acts. Once more the sacraments become important, in this case primarily the sacrament of the altar, the Mass. Here, it is held, each time the Mass is offered, Jesus dies anew, sacrificed once more. When the words of institution in the Mass are spoken, the wine ceases to be wine and becomes blood, the bread ceases to be bread and becomes the true body of Christ. This view is called transubstantiation, or a change of substance. Then when the priest raises high the true body and blood of Jesus, Jesus dies once more, again making substitutionary payment for man's guilt—only this time it is a death for actual guilt, guilt acquired since baptism by the doing of wrong acts, and not for original guilt.

Once more it can be seen that the stress is both objective and backward. Jesus actually dies again, and that death is objectively valid in the eyes of God, accomplishing its purpose, making amends for man's guilt, man's guilt of the past, accumulated in past bad acts. We saw also that the church through the centuries devised many other means of dealing with this accumulation of guilt, such as periods of penance, indulgences granted by the church, and, finally, a period of purgation—time spent in purgatory—in which the last vestiges of actual guilt are burned away.

From all this, it can be seen that the sacraments in the Catholic Church are both important and many. They are many, in addition to baptism and the Mass: marriage, ordination, penance, the last rites, and other rituals as well are seen as sacraments, each of them dealing with actual guilt. And they *are* important. The Catholic Church is a *sacramental* church, placing its emphasis on *God's* act. *God* is the actor in these rites, himself at work accomplishing his ends of atonement. These are *sacraments,* and their efficacy is not dependent on the attitude of the believer or the faith of the officiant, the one performing the ceremony. This problem was faced and the Catholic answer hammered out in the ancient Donatist controversies that wracked the church in its early centuries of life when official doctrine was being formed. What the Donatist controversy boiled down to in simplest terms is precisely that the act was valid and efficacious even if the sacrament was received unworthily or administered by a rascal who was a renegade in the faith. This could be so because the effectiveness of the act rested ultimately not on the individual being acted upon or on the person administering the ritual, but rather it rested on the authority of God who had entrusted to the church at large, and not to any specific individual in the church, that power to perform the sacraments.

From all this flows the Catholic concept of the church. Salvation means to be made right in God's eyes, to have your guilt taken away. And that guilt is taken away by participation in the sacraments. Thus those who administer the sacraments have a peculiar position, a special power. A power, it is true, that is delegated by God and ultimately dependent upon him, but still a power that *is* delegated to those who perform the sacraments. Thus it comes about that the church is an *institutional* concept. The church is not, basically, the sum of all the individuals, lay and clergy alike, who belong to it. Instead, the church consists essentially of those responsible for the administration of the salvation-granting sacraments. The church is the institution, the hierarchy, the priests, bishops, and pope, for they are the ones who stand as God's representatives, mediating salvation to the individual.

There are two kinds of people in the church, two levels of Christianity: there are the priests and there are the laymen. Of these two, it is the priest who stands in the special position, for it is he who administers the sacraments. But to whom much is given, much is expected. Thus there grew up in Catholic thought an emphasis on the Counsels of Perfection. In Matt. 19:12, 21, Jesus is shown as insisting that if anyone "would be perfect," he had to give up all property and wealth on the one hand and, on the other, be a eunuch, chaste, devoid of all sexual experience. It was the priest who stood in this special relationship, who was supposed to be perfect—not the layman, not that much was expected of him. Thus it was the priest who had to take vows of poverty and of celibacy. The emphasis, you see, was on gradation, on levels within the church. Much more was demanded of those who were entrusted with the sacraments: they had to be perfect.

This emphasis on the organizational church, on the members of the hierarchy and their special role, received added weight from several other historical factors that have to be held in mind if we would fully understand just how the Catholic view of the church emerged. Even at the risk, therefore, of wandering too far afield from our basic purpose, we have to glance at least at one or two other men and movements that had influence early in the evolution of the Catholic Church.

In its earliest years, in its first and formative centuries, the Christian religion was almost overwhelmed by another religion called Gnosticism. The whole subject of Gnosticism is so enormously complicated that even to this day scholars are not entirely agreed as to whether this was a perversion of Christian teaching that grew up inside the Christian religion, infecting it from within, or whether it was an external rival religion thrusting in from the outside. That whole complex issue we cannot even enter into here. All we can do is to give the briefest outline of what it was all about and how it affected the church's understanding of itself.

Gnosticism was basically Greek. The ancient Greeks believed that there were two parts to man: body and spirit; and that of the two parts, body was evil and spirit was good. You can see how such a view could come about. Here is a chap who wants to sit with Plato, he on one end of the log and the student on the other end, the two of them having dialogue. There they sit, expounding and explaining the profound and beautiful visions of things spiritual: service, love, self-sacrifice, duty to state, all the marvelous ideals that move the spirit of man. But then, right there in the middle of the moving conversation about self-denial and service, some young girl in a short tunic walks by and immediately all the lofty ideals are dispatched, and the student (and perhaps Plato too) looks after her and lusts after her! The biological impulses of the body interfere with the pursuits of the mind. Flesh is evil, interfering, the root of all temptation; only the mind is good, noble, pure. Or, there they are, one on one end of the log and the other on the other end, talking about justice and democracy, education for all, or some other flowing ideal. And what happens? The student's stomach starts to growl. He has to go home and eat something so he can fill his stomach and make it stop growling. The physical needs of the flesh interfere with the pursuits of the mind. The body is evil; only the mind is good. This is Greek dualism—flesh versus spirit.

Gnosticism was simply this basic Greek idea carried to an extreme. Not only was the body held to be evil, but so also was the whole world. *Everything* that was physical was bad. Gnosticism, beginning with that conviction as its hub, went on from there to challenge and contradict many things that were dear and basic to the early Christian religion. In the first place, obviously, the Old Testament had to be rejected, for, after all, the Old Testament insisted that the world was not evil but good, for does it not say in the Creation story in Genesis, again and again, after each stage of creation, that God backed up and evaluated his creative handiwork by saying of the world, "And it is good . . . and it is good"? Also, does not the psalmist say, "The earth is the LORD's and the fulness thereof"? That emphasis on the physical world as good was totally incompatible with the tenets of Gnosticism, and thus Gnosticism rejected it, actually insisting that there were *two* Gods, or deities, one who created the physical world with all its flaws and lusts, an evil deity, and the other who created the good world of the spirit. The Old Testament was rejected by Gnosticism, denounced and set aside. It was *not* the word of God, for it wrongly evaluated this world of flesh and substance as good.

Also rejected by Gnosticism was the true humanity of Jesus. How could Jesus, good, a savior sent of God, truly be good if he were fleshly, a true human being, part physical? Thus Gnosticism was linked to Docetism, a fancy word that means, simply, a denial of Jesus' humanity. This rejection of Jesus' humanity led to a radical rewriting of basic New Testament passages, or if not to a rewriting of them, at least to a new, novel, and often bizarre interpretation of standard texts. For example, since Jesus was not true man, obviously he could not truly die, for only man, not God, could die. Who then died on the cross? The Gnostics argued that it was not Jesus who died there, it was Simon of Cyrene! Remember that poor chap who was pressed into service and forced to carry the cross when Jesus stumbled and fell, Simon of Cyrene? Well, it was *he* who got himself crucified, Jesus slipping off into the crowd! Or another example of this bizarre interpretation, in a recently discovered Gnostic document, is the startling bit of information that Jesus' mother, Mary, was a man! We can see how, by Gnostic logic, this had to be. Woman was essentially evil. Not only did she lure man sexually, inviting him to revel in the joys of the flesh, an evil undertaking, but even more than that, she bore children. She stuck good spirit into a cage of evil flesh. Woman was evil, and thus Jesus could not have been born of a woman—his mother must have been a man!

We have gone far enough to see the broad outlines of Gnosticism insofar as it concerns us here. It led to a radical reexamination and rejection of the treasured writings of the church. The Gnostics were bringing their own interpretation of significant passages and causing havoc with the literary inherited treasures of the church, setting aside the Old Testament, rejecting some New Testament books, disputing key passages in other New Testament books. It was in this atmosphere that Irenaeus, the Bishop of Lyons, one of the early church fathers, entered into the fray. Among the many other things he did was to insist upon the primacy of all things apostolic—the apostolic canon, the apostolic creed, the apostolic succession. In effect, what he claimed was that the Gnostics were not free to set aside this or that book as they wished, making up the Bible out of whichever books they favored. Instead, the church was heir to and based upon the writings and insights of the apostles, determined by and indebted to the writings produced by and accepted by the original disciples, those who had been with Jesus.

Jesus and the apostles accepted the Old Testament; Jesus even preached out of it. Thus the Gnostics could not set the Old Testament aside. The apostles, the men who had been with Jesus, wrote down what they had seen and heard—exactly, it was believed, as they had seen it and heard it. Thus the apostolic writings, the books of the New Testament—Matthew, Mark, Luke, and John, the letters of Paul and the epistles of Peter and James, the Apocalypse of John—all these apostolic writings had to be accepted and could not be set aside to satisfy the whims or the peculiar views of some wild-eyed Gnostic. This was the first great contribution of Irenaeus, the establishment of the canon. "Canon" is simply a Greek word that means "measuring rod," or, by extension, "ultimate authority, that by which man is measured." And that by which the church was measured, its ultimate authority, was the canon —the writings produced by (the New Testament) or accepted by (the Old Testament) the earliest apostles.

But this was only the first step in the struggle with Gnosticism. So all right, now the church had a bundle of books to which it was bound, by which it was measured, the canon. But who was to *interpret* those books? After all, being what they are, men can wring just about any meaning they want to out of a written page. Some summary of the *meaning* of those books had to be arrived at or else anyone could make them mean whatever he wished them to mean. This led Irenaeus to argue for an apostolic creed, for a rule of faith, a summary of the meaning of the Scriptures as the apostles saw them. Irenaeus argued that not only were the *books* but likewise what the books *meant* inherited from the apostolic age.

There was latent in those books a basic point of view that could be summarized and formulated and that has come to be known as the Apostles' Creed. Here, in these brief statements, is given the church's position on all the points disputed by the Gnostics. Notice, for example, that the first article, "I believe in God the Father Almighty, Maker of heaven and earth," rejects the Gnostic view that the world is evil, a product of an inferior God. Not at all! It is the handiwork of the Father, a good creation. Notice how the second article, the extended discussion of the person of Jesus, refutes all the Gnostic claims. First of all, he was *not* born of a man! He was "born of the Virgin Mary." His true humanity is affirmed. It was not Simon of Cyrene who was crucified. Rather, it was Jesus who was "crucified, dead, and buried."

But even after arguing for a *regula fides*, a "rule of faith," a creed dating back to the apostles, Irenaeus' work was not yet done. It was clear that not all the four Gospels always agreed exactly with one another. The Gospel of John, for example, seems to say that the cleansing of the Temple by Jesus took place at the outset of his ministry, three years before his death. The other three Gospels, however, seem to argue that the cleansing took place the last week of Jesus' life, just a matter of days before his crucifixion. If the original apostles could sometimes seem to disagree, it also followed, logically, that those who interpreted the books could also disagree. The interpretation of the books was left open to anyone, it would seem. But here was the third link in Irenaeus' argument. The interpretation was *not* left open to just anyone. The original interpretation belonged to the apostles who created the creed, and after them, the interpretation belonged to the successors of the apostles, the bishops of the church.

But what of those instances when the bishops themselves did not all agree? Who then had the last word? Here the seeds of apostolic succession were sown, the seeds of the papacy. The heirs of the apostles were the bishops. They were responsible for proper interpretation in their day, even as the apostles were responsible in an earlier day. But even the apostles had a head, a leader, a man who stood in a preeminent position. That man was Peter. Thus, logically, Peter's successor likewise had a pre-eminent position. The pope, the bishop of Rome, stood as the final arbiter or judge of what the Christian faith meant. This stress on the role of the pope did not, of course, spring forth full-grown in Irenaeus' day, but the seeds were planted then. The day was now in sight, thanks to Irenaeus' arguments, that when the assembled bishops of the church met and disagreed, unable to decide on the precise meaning of a given passage, the word of the pope, the successor of Peter, would be final.

Against this backdrop of early controversy and struggle with the Gnostics we can see how it came about that this organiza-tional or hierarchical structure of the church, which we noted earlier, came to the fore. Of course the priest, the bishop, the pope, each had a special and important role, a rung above the layman! They were the final arbiters of the meaning of the faith. Their prime position, their unique role, was established. They had to be obeyed—or else the result would be religious anarchy, spiritual chaos, a lack of discipline and authority in which each went his own way, deciding for himself what he believed, how he would put that belief into practice, and which books or parts of the Bible he would accept as authoritative. Such diversity could mean only confusion and eventually disas-ter and decay. It is easy to see how, against that early historical background, the belief arose that the clergy had a prime and special role, and that the ordinary layman, outside the super-structure of the organized church, had to obey, else all was lost.

But it is equally easy to see that this historical movement, so necessary in the light of those turbulent early days, was bound to produce a reaction. What these views of Irenaeus really did, in actual fact, was to limit the role of the Holy Spirit. No longer was it believed that each and every member of the church had immediate access to God, illuminated individually by the Holy Spirit. On the contrary, the illuminating work of the Holy Spirit was limited, on the one hand, to his activity in the past, when he inspired the prophets and apostles to write what they did and interpret the way they did, and, on the other hand, limited to the pope and bishops in the present, who applied the other truths to the new times. The Holy Spirit, it was believed, was no longer spread wholesale or in blanket fashion over the whole of the church. He was active in the compilation of the Scriptures and in the clergy who interpreted the Scriptures. But he was not active in any powerful or significant way in the life of the individual layman. The individual layman was not to lean on direct divine illumination, but instead to lean on instruction from the bishop.

It was inevitable that such a view, vitally necessary as it was in those early troubled days of struggle with Gnosticism, would lead to a reaction, to a renewed insistence that each and every Christian was open to direction, in an unmediated way, by the Holy Spirit. The shackling of the Spirit, the tying of his activity to a book of the past and to the hierarchy of the present, would be resisted. And resisted it was when Montanism exploded on the scene, shortly after Irenaeus.

Montanism, like Gnosticism, is an enormously complicated phenomenon, too complex to be exhausted in any discussion here. We limit ourselves only to those concepts of it which concern us immediately. Sitting on a barren hillock in Asia Minor, a man named Montanus, an enthusiastic personality (we would probably call him psychic if we wanted to be kindly or psychotic if we preferred to be harsh) read John 15:26, a key verse for his movement, and concluded that in his day this promised Counselor, the Holy Spirit, had come, and had born full and final witness to all things. Montanus believed that he was the mouthpiece of God, a prophet inspired of the Spirit, able to speak with authority equal to and even superior to the decrees of the official church. The Holy Spirit was not shackled but poured out anew. Coupled with this conviction of a new outpouring of the Spirit was the belief that the end of the age was at hand, that all human history was hastening to a close, and that the need was great for a self-disciplined, ascetic way of life. Punish yourself now, purify yourself in the present hour, and thus be prepared for the approaching Kingdom, escaping out of purgatory.

Thus it was that Montanism as a movement gathered together all kinds of strange bedfellows. On the one hand, it appealed to the visionary types, to those of an ecstatic or emotional nature like Montanus himself, who heard voices and believed that the Spirit worked directly upon him. The movement also appealed to the apocalyptic people, those who yearned for the end of the world. But also, and most especially, it appealed to the ascetics, to the self-punishing ones, who wanted to purge themselves of all guilt right here and right now through monkish practices that would prepare them to go straight to heaven when the new world came, by purging them in the immediate moment, through rigorous self-discipline, of their actual guilt. Incidentally, this is why Tertullian joined the movement, for, as we saw earlier, he was a harsh and legal man who saw sin as guilt that had to be dealt with in harsh and legal ways.

This appeal of Montanism was especially powerful because, during the period of which we are now speaking, a certain laxity had spread over the church. Persecutions had exploded on the church. The Romans had attacked it, trying to wipe it out. Many had stood firm, but many others had recanted the faith, giving up their allegiance to save their necks. Thus when the persecutions ended, the church had a problem—what to do with the lapsed, those who had backed down in the face of crisis.

There were those who had argued for harsh and stringent measures. Damn them, leave them to remain outside the church that they had left, for apostasy was a *mortal* sin, the sin against the Holy Spirit, the unforgivable sin for which there was no cure. Others argued for a more lenient view, claiming that, under the circumstances, the renunciation of the faith was to be seen as a *venial* sin, forgivable, able to be overcome through proper penance and self-discipline. Eventually, it was the more lenient position that prevailed. It had to prevail, in one sense, because the number of lapsed was so great that to be harsh appeared equivalent to dealing the church a deathblow through losing such a large proportion of its members. A certain sense of tolerance, a willingness to settle for less than total consecration, became the mood of the official church. It was at this point of time that the Counsels of Perfection, mentioned earlier, became exceedingly important. The priests, the bishops, *they* had to be perfect, but for the ordinary rank and file something less than full obedience and perfection was acceptable.

Against all of this—the shackling of the Holy Spirit to the past, the tendency to be lenient—Montanism reacted, insisting that the same high standards were demanded of *all* believers, for all were under the direct influence of the Holy Spirit. The organized or official church was in a dilemma. Which way to go? To denounce Montanism as a schismatic heresy, a false teaching, would be equivalent to rejecting the Holy Spirit on the one hand, and advocating a kind of second-level Christian life on the other in which laxity was not only forgiven but even tolerated and implicitly encouraged. To approve Montanism, however, could be equally disastrous, for that would mean an abandonment of all that Irenaeus had accomplished: a loss of a center of authority, the opening of the door to individualism, and then to anarchy where everyone went his own way. Which way to go?

The choice was not easy, and the hesitancy of the church to take an immediate stand because of the gravity of the issues involved was entirely understandable. Eventually and reluctantly the church was forced to make its decision, and Montanism was condemned. Indeed, in one sense it had to be, for to allow the view to continue that each and every person had a direct pipeline to heaven, each personally filled with direct divine communication given by the Holy Spirit, would be to open the door which had just been slammed shut in the struggle against Gnosticism to anarchy and chaos. Montanism was condemned, and this condemnation of Montanism was one of the most formative and fundamental facts in the evolution of the Catholic Church. All the earlier tendencies were reaffirmed, and seeds once planted now flowered. The organizational or institutional view of the church was affirmed. A two-layer Christianity, priests and laymen, became an established fact. For the priests, the standards were high; they had to take the vows, adhere to the Counsels of Perfection, swear to be chaste and to be poor. Greater latitude was allowed the layman because not so much was given to him.

The role of the clergy, both its interpretive function and its role as mediator between God and the layman, became primary. It came to be held as an axiom of the church that there could be no salvation outside the church, that is, outside the official structure. Salvation was obtained through the sacraments, through the penances and indulgences and eventual purgatory argued for by the church. Sin was guilt, and guilt was dealt with only through baptism and the Mass and the other sacraments administered by the priests. It was not accidental but inevitable that the man who followed Tertullian and called him "master" would be the man who would be the first to argue that there was no salvation outside the organized church. It was Cyprian who first said *extra ecclesiam nulla salus* ("outside the church, no salvation").

This is the point of view, the comprehension of the nature of the church and the role of the sacraments, which prevailed for centuries, down to the time of the Protestant Reformation. But then, a new view of sin demanded the formulation of a new view of the church. By way of brief summary, it can be seen that the church was essentially an institution, not a bundle of believers. The sacraments were objective, acts of God, *ex opere operato*, that is, valid in their own right because their authority depended, not on the individual's faith, but on the authority delegated by God first to the apostles and then to the apostles' successors, the bishops and the pope. Faith was not a personal commitment to or identification with the immediate intervention of the Holy Spirit. Rather, it was obedience to the church officials to whom the Holy Spirit's activities were limited. Indeed, that could even be seen as a synonym for the word "faith." The term meant "faithfulness," in the sense of obedience to the hierarchy.

From this moment on, as a careful study of the later Trinitarian councils reveals, the Holy Spirit was a secondary issue, a doctrine of relatively little importance. The Trinitarian struggles are, in fact, poorly named, for they were not *tri*nitarian at all, not at all concerned with the *three* persons of the Godhead, but instead they were basically concerned with *two* persons— with the Father and the Son, their relationship—and the dogmas and doctrines concerning the Spirit were added on at the end of the struggles almost as an afterthought.

All the views just looked at, the concept of the church, the nature of the sacraments, the definition of faith, the role of the Spirit—all of these can be traced back to the one basic starting point, the conviction that sin is guilt. This basic starting point was strengthened by the unrolling of the historical struggles we have already indicated, but the fact still remains that all these views of the Catholic Church, in one way or another, can be traced back to its concept of sin. Sin is guilt. This basic conviction was challenged by the Protestant Reformation, and out of this challenge there arose new concepts as to what constituted the church, the role and nature of the sacraments, and the relationship of the individual believer to the Holy Spirit.

In examining these new views we begin not with the man who touched off the Reformation or revolution, Luther, but rather with that element which went farther than Luther—the enthusiasts, or Anabaptists, or Pentecostals. Call them by whichever name you prefer, but they represent a specific point of view quite different from what preceded them. For them, sin was not an objective bundle of accumulated guilt. For them, sin was not a concrete mountain standing as barrier between man and God—a barrier of guilt standing even after man repented. Instead, sin was for them rebellion. And, as such, sin was seen as intensely *personal*, intensely *subjective*.

Subjective—that is, the only thing standing between man and God was man's own attitude. God was not angry, he was love, and, like the loving father in the parable of the prodigal, if the wayward runaway would come home, he would find the door standing wide, no obstacles in the way, no penance to make, no suffering to undergo. Sin was rebellion, subjective rebellion—that and that alone separated man from God. Thus when the rebellion was gone, when man's subjective attitude was altered, the separation too was gone, and the fatted calf could be killed and there would be rejoicing, for that which was lost was found again.

And sin also was personal, personal in that no one could repent for the runaway son, no one could represent him, no one could suffer in his place or make things right in his stead. It was *his* rebellion; thus it had to be *his* repentance. It was *his* subjective attitude that was wrong and needed altering, and altering it would have to be an intensely personal act that no one could perform in his place.

Given these ideas as starting points, it is easy to see how all the emphases of this wing of the Christian church come forward. In the first place, as we noted earlier, the only Christian denomination that takes as its name one of the sacraments, the Baptists, do not believe in baptism, at least not in the classical tradition. For them, baptism is not *ex opere operato*, an act of God in itself, bringing forth its own fruit independently of any attitude of or alteration in man. Infant baptism is not only unpracticed, it is anathema to a good Baptist. How could it be otherwise? If sin is seen as rebellion and its answer is seen as repentance, then how could an infant rebel, much less repent for that rebellion? It cannot be done, and thus infant baptism remains unpracticed. It is only when sin is seen as an objective fact, as opposed to a subjective attitude, that infant baptism can be practiced.

The Catholic Church sees sin as objective, that is, original guilt that is inherited. The main-line Protestant churches, such as Lutheran, Episcopalian, and Presbyterian, also see sin as objective, that is, as bondage, a condition from which man must be set free. For both of those wings, therefore, infant baptism is not only possible but vitally necessary. But not for the Pente-

costal or Baptist wing of the church. Their view of sin as subjective rebellion will not allow it. Even with adults, their view
of baptism is different from that found in other denominations.
For Lutherans and Catholics alike, baptism remains an act of
God, the stress being on what *he* does, not on how man feels.
It *is* a sacrament, a divine act, and not simply a symbolic outward expression of how a man feels inside.

But for the Baptist group, baptism is but an outward symbol
of an inward change. Man washes himself on the outside with
water as a summary and symbol of the internal change in his
own attitude. He has made himself clean. He has set aside his
rebellion. Like the prodigal, he has ceased running to a far
country and has come home. This renewed filial attitude is
symbolized by the washing in the water. To express this spa-
tially one could say that for the Catholic Church, baptism is a
downward arrow, an act of God, God coming to man and dealing with objective guilt. But for the Baptist segment of the
church, baptism is an upward arrow, man coming to God, re-
penting and promising to be better. The renewing power of the
ritual lies not in the intervention of God but in the attitude of
man. Hence no infant baptism; for a child, an infant, can have
no such right attitude, being too young either to sin or to be
sorry for sin.

Because sin is rebellion—personal and subjective, to be dealt
with only personally and subjectively—we come to a whole
different attitude toward the church. Salvation is not to be
found in the administration of some liturgical rite, the partak-
ing of the Supper or something like that. As a matter of fact, in
actual practice, there is practically no theology of the sacrament of the altar in these denominations. It was Luther and
Zwingli who locked in combat over the proper interpretation
of the Supper, and it was against the Catholic interpretation of
the Mass that Luther railed. There the argument unrolled and
continues to unroll among Catholics, Calvinists, and Lutherans,
for to them the sacrament deals with sin as an objective fact,
either as guilt or as bondage. But with the Anabaptist element,
sin is rebellion, dealt with only by repentance and not by ritual

or church ceremony, and consequently the interpretation of the Supper, indeed, even concern with the Supper, was never a matter of burning concern. In a word, the Pentecostal or Baptist view of sin made the sacraments irrelevant.

Because the sacraments themselves were not charged with the power unto salvation, those who administered them were less exalted, less significant. Never in Pentecostal circles has a powerful hierarchy arisen as has been the case in Catholic history. Or to put the same issue into different words: since my sin is personal and subjective, and I stand solely responsible before God, called to account for my individual hostility; no one else can intercede for me. As in the parable, the elder brother must stand on the sidelines; he can neither contribute nor take away anything as my father and I are reconciled. There is no mediator, no in-between priest figure standing midway between me and God. I am in an immediate and personal relationship with God, and the church loses its importance as a mediating agency measuring out to me satisfaction for guilt through prescribed ritual.

It is a matter of incontrovertible historical fact that the idea of a centrally organized church has never been popular in Baptist and Pentecostal circles. To this day the Baptist churches are not a national church in the usual sense of that word. Instead, they are a federation of individual congregations, banding together for the more expedient execution of common purposes. The decisions of the national federation are in no way whatever binding on individual congregations. They remain autonomous and independent, for the basic emphasis of the entire denomination is intensely personal. In the light of their view of sin it cannot be otherwise. Neither responsibility nor authority can be delegated by the individual, who stands sole and responsible before God.

On the other hand, if the role of the sacraments and of the institutional church is minimized, the importance of the Holy Spirit is stressed (as is clear, obviously, in the very name of one of the groups of this wing, the Pentecostals, who thus incorporate into their very title the celebration of the spilling out of the Spirit on the day of Pentecost). In direct opposition to the Catholic Church, which, on the one hand, stresses the centrality of the sacraments and the clergy who administer them and, on the other hand, disregards or minimizes the idea of direct and personal communication with God outside the ecclesiastical structure through the Holy Spirit, the Pentecostal Church stresses the dynamic and direct role of the Holy Spirit. Many of the same emphases seen in the ancient Montanist movement—such as a stress on the return of Christ, a demand for greater personal piety, purity, and self-discipline, but, most especially, an insistence upon a real and deeply felt personal experience of the Holy Spirit—appear anew in this segment of the church today, and appear for precisely the same reasons that produced the Montanist movement in the first place.

The Baptist or Pentecostal movement was and remains a protest against what could be called cold clericalism, a sacramental system that reduces a right relationship to God down to a mechanical bookkeeping entry in a divine ledger. At best, the Catholic stress on guilt has a profound and vital insight into the nature of man and the nature of sin. It shouts out with compelling power that man's wrong deeds have an enduring effect, that even when we turn over a new leaf the wounds of our acts run red and sore, that even when our hostility ends, others as well as ourselves remain hurt, and hurt badly. At worst, however, the Catholic stress on guilt can encourage the concept of religion as a dues-paying gesture in a Christian club. So many acts of penance or contrition, and the slate is wiped clean, and I am free to proceed as before, bumbling along as I will, quite assured that my future bumblings, like my past errors, can be dealt with through the sacramental system.

Such a system, or such a misconception of the system (for that is what it is, a misconception), encourages laxity on the one hand and produces a deadened sensitivity on the other. It was against this that the left wing of the Reformation reacted, insisting as it did and as it does on an intensely personal and subjective relationship with God, unmediated through the church, but instead direct and alive, infused with the living presence of the Spirit. It has always been this wing of the church which has stressed glossolalia, speaking in tongues, that ecstatic emotional experience in which the Spirit sweeps upon an individual, transporting him, as a necessary or at least encouraging proof that God is truly present in his life.

We have, then, two views of sin: as objective guilt or as subjective rebellion, Catholic and Pentecostal, each with its own differing views of what the church is and what the role of the sacraments is to be, and how important the Holy Spirit is. For one, faith can well be translated "faithfulness," obedience to the bishop, subjugation to the ecclesiastical superstructure. To the other, the Pentecostal wing, faith could be better defined as "intensely personal commitment," the resolve to do better, the translation of hostility toward God into obedience to him.

But different as these two Christian systems are, with their radically clashing views of the church and of the sacraments and the role of the Spirit, they are, nonetheless, united on one point. Sin is of man. It is either an act of man, rebellion, or it is the consequence of that act, guilt. Either way, it is something for which responsible man is held to account. Man is always and without fail seen as free and self-determining, able by his own efforts to perform what is required of him. That he does not is what in the one case constitutes his rebellion, in the other case his guilt.

Luther begins with an entirely different point of departure, seeing man not as free but as helpless, seeing sin not as an act but as a condition, a condition of bondage from which God and God alone can set man free. This view led to a quite different comprehension of the nature of the sacraments, the nature of the church, and the role of the Spirit.

For Luther, as for the Catholic Church, baptism was an objective act. The stress was on the divine intervention, not on the human attitude. The arrow was downward. It was a true sacrament, valid in its own right, accomplishing something quite independently of any internal response in man. Thus the act could be performed even on infants. Although Luther agreed on all those ideas with the Catholic Church, he disagreed on another essential point. For him, the emphasis was not a *backward* look, the discharge of a past debt, the end of an older way of life. For Luther, the look was *forward*. Nothing old ended. Rather, something new began. To put it a different way and to stretch language a little in doing so, in Catholic teaching, baptism did not change man's *condition*, only his *status*. That is, man was always free, both before and after baptism, always accountable for his wrong deeds because he was always seen as able to refrain from bad deeds. As we saw, concupiscence was understood as *tending* toward sin but not as sin itself. The tendency could be resisted, the wrong deed avoided, man could refrain from sin. Nothing was changed in this condition of man due to the act of baptism.

What did change was man's status. There were, as we saw, two kinds of guilt held against our account, original and actual. Original—that was the taint of the race, the contamination we inherited. My father has red hair, so I have red hair. But having red hair does not make me more or less responsible! I may be stained and smeared by the guilt of the race at the time of my birth, but I am not as a consequence helpless or crippled. Red hair makes me look different, but it does not affect my psychic or spiritual capacities, reducing me to bondage. Nor does this inherited guilt reduce me to bondage. It is a legal mark, not a psychological one. It renders me guilty but not enslaved. Even before baptism, I am responsible. But, according to Catholic thought, baptism wipes away the stain, dyes the hair color other than blood-red, pronounces me innocent of inherited guilt. My status is changed, a past debt discharged, but my condition remains the same. An old mark, the mark of Cain, is wiped away.

For Luther the situation was entirely different. Man was born in a condition of slavery, helpless under the devil, a beast of burden made to be ridden. Even after baptism man remained a slave! Nothing ended! Instead, something new was added. As of baptism, a new force, a new power, was added to the human equation; another condition was laid alongside the older condition. Man was now no longer under the exclusive dominion of Satan; he was also under the influence of the Holy Spirit. They were not successive states but simultaneous ones. Man, as of baptism, led a dual existence—*simul iustus et peccator*, "simultaneously a saint and a sinner," at one and the same time under the devil and yet a servant of God. This divided existence continued until the end of life. Reflecting the language of Rom., ch. 7, where the apostle Paul saw the Christian life as a continuing warfare going on until death, Luther too saw the Christian life, begun at baptism, in those terms of continuing conflict. Once baptized, the old way of life, the old Adam, did not end but was, instead, added to, and man in addition to being under Satan was now also under God, a split personality, a Jekyll and Hyde, seeing, as it were, "a war within his members" producing a cry of near-despair, "Wretched man that I am! Who will deliver me?" (Rom. 7:23–24).

Different as Catholic and Baptist conceptions may be, at one place they are alike. Both see life unrolling in two stages, prebaptismal and postbaptismal. In one case, original guilt was discharged and individual accountability for wrong deeds began. In the other case, personal hostility ended, symbolized by external washing, and personal consecration began. But for Luther life was a *three*-stage affair. Before baptism, man was solely and exclusively a slave of the devil, a lost and condemned creature. In heaven, in the world beyond, man would be exclusively under God. But in this world, after baptism, the Christian lived under both Satan and God. The old condition of servitude was not ended but supplemented, added to. Baptism, then, had a forward look. It marked the beginning of this new life in tension, life to be lived out under the Holy Spirit and the evil spirit. Man, from this moment on, became responsible, though not responsible to work out his own salvation in fear and trembling but rather responsible to submit to the Holy Spirit, who would accomplish what man by himself could not. The stress was not on what man could do. Even as a baptized Christian, man was bound in sin, for sin was a continuing condition and only God could bring forth the good life. All that

37426

man did was not of his own efforts but due instead to the intervention of the Spirit.

Luther had no doctrine of sanctification, no belief that man could make progress in personal perfection, improving himself through greater individual efforts. (It was precisely this *failure* by Luther to improve himself, despite a program of self-discipline so rigorous that it broke his health and ruined his stomach, which caused Luther to conclude that current Catholic teachings were wrong. It forced him to search for new answers, a search that resulted in the Reformation.) Instead, Luther argued that everything which was brought forth in the life of the baptized Christian was not the product of personal endeavor but rather the gift of the Spirit, who worked in man as of baptism. And at this point, Luther, a Pauline scholar, had many Pauline passages to which he could point. He would point to a passage such as Gal. 5:22–23 and remark that Paul here says that all the virtues of the Christian life, "love, joy, peace, patience, kindness, goodness, faith [not "faithfulness," as the RSV wrongly translates; the word in the Greek is *pistis*, "faith"], gentleness, self-control"—all these things were not the products of man's efforts but rather the "fruit of the Spirit." Luther could point to Rom. 8:26 where Paul insists that the Spirit even forms our prayers for us, for we do not even know how to pray as we ought. He could point to I Cor. 12:3 or Eph. 2:8 where Paul flatly insists that not even faith is an individual accomplishment, an act of man, but is instead a gift of God, his creation, due to his intervention, an utterance of allegiance produced in us by the Holy Spirit.

Perhaps the best way to comprehend Luther's ideas on this issue is to examine what he meant by faith. It was *not* an act of man, but something that God produced in man, through the Spirit, if man but submitted to that Spirit. Luther defined faith in terms of three Latin words. The first is *notitia*, "knowledge." Faith is not an emotional ecstasy bubbling up out of the liver like some gaseous vapor. Instead, it is knowledge, grounded in historical fact. Faith is not a warm mystical experience that makes man glow, but is instead anchored in history, and a knowledge of that history is demanded to make faith a reality. Jesus was a true historical figure who was, as the Nicene Creed says, "crucified under Pontius Pilate." Pilate was an actual historical person, Jesus' death took place at a datable moment in human history. Knowledge of that history is vital. Without that knowledge or *notitia* there is no faith.

But faith is more than knowledge. The second word Luther used was *assensus,* that is, "agreement with," or "acknowledgment of," the accuracy of that historical information. In this sense, faith could be seen as intellectual agreement with, or acknowledgment of, the accuracy of that historical information. In this sense, faith could be seen as a nodding of the head "yes," the endorsement of a series of propositions. The individual had to agree that those facts as taught by the church were valid and real. Being instructed was not sufficient. He had to agree with that instruction, accept it as true. But even this was not the core of faith. A man could have all knowledge, memorize the Bible from cover to cover and be able to say the Lord's Prayer backward in his sleep, but this, even when coupled with intellectual assent, was not the essential of faith.

The heart of faith for Luther was found in the third Latin word *fiducia.* That word could be translated "heartfelt trust" or "total commitment." Here was the heart of faith. By way of explanation, I am going to use a story our seminary professor told my class some years ago. I have never heard a better illustration. When he was a young man, first married, all the newlyweds went to Niagara Falls on their honeymoon. Back in those days before television, entertainment was found in the wandering carnivals that went across our land. While my professor was there at Niagara Falls, a carnival came to town, and one of the acts was a tightrope walker. A line was strung across the Falls, and an acrobat wandered out on it. When he first began his act (it was early in the season), he almost stumbled and fell. But, as the act went on, he regained his old form, and by the end of the performance the acrobat was practically running across the wire. Finally, at the last triumphant moment, he wheeled out a wheelbarrow and asked the audience if they thought he could push a human being across the Falls on the barrow. "You could push an elephant across in the wheelbarrow!" they all replied. "You are the greatest tightrope walker who ever lived!" they all exclaimed. "All right, then," he asked, "who wants to climb in?" No takers! They had *notitia*, knowledge of his skills. With their own eyes they had seen him perform. And they had *assensus*, for they all agreed that he could do it. But no one had *fiducia*. No one had the heartfelt trust, the total commitment, the willingness to confide his whole being into the hands of another. None dared to be wheeled across the chasm, trusting solely and exclusively not in their own power but in the skill of another. It would not be their doing, but his, and this was asking too much. Faith is like that. It is not simply the accumulation of information or the intellectual endorsement of data obtained. It is climbing into the wheelbarrow, putting your whole life at the disposition of a power outside yourself. It is not man's act, but trust in God's action.

Even with this illustration, Luther's view of faith is not complete, for our illustration has one glaring weakness. While it stresses the need for total commitment, that total commitment wrongly appears to originate in a resolve of man's, in his willingness to climb into the barrow. Not so for Luther. Another illustration: Modern psychology has now concluded that when a child is born, that child is able to hate with every fiber of its existence. It can hate, but it cannot love. It cannot love until it has first been loved. This is Sigmund Freud's "vessel" theory. Simply enough, it states that you cannot pour water out of a vessel until, well, until what? Until you first pour water into it! You cannot pour love out of a person; a child, a newborn, cannot love until he has first been loved. The child who has never been loved is unable to love, unable to show loyalty toward law or respect for others, literally unable, until he has first been loved. The child who is unloved is hurled toward wrongdoing, unable to do otherwise. The courts even have a term to express such a condition, "compulsive delinquent," *compelled* toward evil. But fondling speaks its own language.

As a child is nurtured and nourished, treasured by a parent, love is poured in and emancipation is accomplished. He becomes able to love in return.

Now, the important thing to note is not the psychology illustration in itself, for in the fast-moving world of psychiatry and psychology this conviction might change. But whether it changes in psychology or not is beside the point, for it remains a truth of Biblical teaching: "For this is love, not that we first loved him, but that he first loved us" (I John 4:10, 19). Our love, our total trust in God, our allegiance to him, is not the product of our own activity. Instead, it is his creation, pulled out of us, poured into us, by exposure to his love. No child sits down on his eleventh birthday and logically decides that from that day onward he will start loving his parents. Love, trust, commitment, allegiance—these are not volitional acts. They are not products of human resolve or intellectual decision. The child of eleven does not say to himself, "Well, here is another birthday, and the folks have come through for me once more, so I guess I should start loving them in return." He does not muse over the fact that whenever he skinned his knee he was embraced or whenever his corduroy pants were torn a new pair was purchased. He does not rationally examine the evidence and then decide on that basis to turn on the spigot of love and allow the flow of his affection. Not at all.

Love is pulled out of him, created in him, independently produced quite apart from his own resolve, made possible not by any mental or volitional activity on his part but created in him by the fact that he was exposed to the love of his parents, which came first. This is the way Luther understood *fiducia*, the heart of faith. It was not man's act but God's creation, produced by His intervention. It was not man's act, because man was enslaved: "I believe that *I cannot* by my own reason or strength believe in Jesus Christ except by the Holy Spirit." Faith is God's act because man, even baptized, is a sinner, a slave of the evil one. Man's condition, after baptism, is a precarious life lived in tension. He is still under Satan but now under God as well, and his responsibility is simply to sub-

mit to the Holy Spirit, to remain passively exposed to the intervention of God, who will bring forth all that is needed. This
is why Luther had no doctrine of sanctification, and why he
could use the phrase "Faith Alone" and "God Alone" interchangeably, because only faith—total trust, committing one's
life to God and being wheeled across the chasm in the barrow—could save, but it was God himself who created that
trust by exposing us to his love. This is why Luther insisted
that the word must be preached in season and out. He did not
argue for evangelistic altar calls, personal resolve, pleading
with men to turn over a new leaf and come forward at a revival
meeting. Instead, he insisted that the word must be preached
and it would of its own efficacy bring forth the new response
of total trust, of *fiducia*.

It can be seen, upon reflection, that in one sense Luther's
position is middle of the road, lying somewhere in between
the two views we earlier examined. The Catholic Church
stresses the objective side of things, God's intervention. So does
Luther. The Baptist group stresses the subjective side of things,
man's response. So does Luther. But in both cases, alongside
the likenesses there are differences. It is an objective act of
God, baptism accomplishes something, and it brings about a
new condition. It places man under the influence of the Spirit.
It does not wipe out a past debt but begins a new life. The
look is forward. It is also subjective. It demands a response.
But it is not a response of individual man, free and unfettered. It is a response created by the Spirit active in Word and
Sacrament. Man's duty is not active, but passive. He is called
to submit to this new power active in him who will do all.

This basic conviction of Luther determined his views on the
sacrament of the altar, the nature of the church, and the role
of the Spirit. Since new life was begun in baptism, that new
life had to be fed, sustained. And so it was in the Lord's Supper. The stress in this ritual for Luther was not on a reenacted
death of Christ, he being put to death anew to cover actual
guilt, but rather the stress was on *communion*, fellowship,
Christ with us in the immediate hour, sustaining us and hold-

ing us up with his strength because our own was insufficient. For the Catholic Church it was essential that the bread and the wine actually be or become the body of Christ, for how else could Christ be put to death anew unless he was actually and physically there? Thus came into being the doctrine of transubstantiation. But for Luther, *cons*ubstantiation was sufficient. Christ was *with* the substance of bread and wine, truly present "in, with, and under" the bread and wine. It was enough, since the emphasis was on Christ's sustaining fellowship rather than on his repeated death, that Jesus simply *be with* the elements rather than *be* the elements.

The sacraments were important, then, and not to be minimized or made irrelevant, as in the Baptist wing. And, since the sacraments were important, creating this new life and feeding it, the church which performed those sacraments was likewise important and not to be minimized. Here too the Lutheran position is somewhat middle of the road. Neither is the organizational church neglected, as in the Pentecostal wing; nor is it exalted, as in the Catholic concept. It is vital. The true church is the place where the word is rightly preached and the sacraments rightly administered, for those are the means, the avenues, of grace, the road by which this power of God reaches us. But there is no special dignity or importance attached to the clergy. They, like the laymen, are likewise all the days of their life *simul iustus et peccator*, sinners as well as saints. They have no special status. There is no double-level Christianity with Counsels of Perfection for some and lesser demands on others. The same trust required of one party is required of the other. Indeed, if there is any one place where Luther dramatically disagreed with the Catholic teachings that preceded him, it is here. For him, there was no such thing as a division between priest and people. *All* were priests, and the concept of the priesthood of *all* believers was basic to both Calvin and Luther.

It was not the administrator of the sacraments or the ordained clergy alone who received a special call from God. All were called. The term "call" or "call of God" has always had a peculiarly important place in Christian terminology. We speak of a man "called" to be a pastor, and enrolling at the seminary. A congregation without a pastor "calls" a man to come to minister to them. But both Luther and Calvin pointed out that the term "call" comes from the Latin word *vocare*, and from that same Latin word comes another word "vocation." The point? We all have a call, we all have a vocation, a profession, a job. It is not just the pastor or priest with the turned-around collar who receives a summons from God, but each and every Christian is called of God and sent forth to serve. Not all are called to the same service, for not all receive the same gifts.

Luther, a Pauline scholar, leaned on I Cor. 12:4 ff. where Paul speaks of the fact that the Holy Spirit gives us a variety of gifts, each of us being endowed in different ways. One has a talent for healing, one a talent for preaching, another for teaching, and so on the list goes in that chapter. But the heart of Paul's thought, picked up by Luther, is that each of us with our individual gifts are *all* called to minister to "the common good" (v. 7). Whatever talents we have are all to be spilled out in service for others. The word "minister," used to describe the role of the clergy in contemporary parlance, is a Latin translation of the Greek word *diakonos*, a word meaning, literally, "table waiter." When the deacons, the *diakonoi*, are chosen in the book of The Acts, their task is to wait on tables. The point is that the housewife who runs herself gray at an early age making meals, washing diapers, and waiting on table is, in Biblical language, every bit as much a minister as is the man who climbs into the pulpit on Sunday morning to preach to the people. They are both called, they both have gifts—different gifts, different talents, different forms of service, but alike in that both of them are equipped of God with peculiar talents which are to be spilled out in service of "the common good."

One of the most famous stories concerning Luther is the tale of the shoemaker who was deeply moved by hearing Luther preach. He asked Luther what he must do, now that God had seized him. "What do you do now?" Luther asked.

"I make shoes" was the answer. "In that case," insisted Luther, "go home and make better shoes. That is your work and your worship!" Basic to that simple response by Luther was the all-pervading conviction that each person who is part of the body of Christ has unique talents and gifts given to him by God which are to be exercised in the specific vocation or calling in which God has placed him. There is no special role for the clergy. They are called, but so are all other Christians, for the church is the priesthood of *all* believers.

Again, it ought be clear how this stream of thought represents a mediating position, emphasizing neither the organizational nor the institutional church, which confines God's activity to the ordained clergy, nor does it go to Pentecostal extremes, which emphasize the individual to such an extent that the larger church pales into insignificance. Luther too stressed the individual, as do the Baptists, but he stressed the individual as part of the body of Christ, as only one part of the larger entity, the church. Proceeding on in I Cor., ch. 12, Luther saw that Paul, although affirming individuality in insisting that each was endowed differently, went on to affirm interdependence as well. No part of the body of Christ can live as an island unto itself. The "rugged individualism" of Luther's attitude has been grossly misunderstood. For him, there was no such thing as a Robinson Crusoe Christian, able to survive in isolation. A body divided and fragmented is a dying body, torn asunder, bleeding to death, doomed. Individualism can be extinction and inevitably will be without the sustaining fellowship of the larger church, without the support of the other members of the body of Christ. This is why Luther had to be thrown out of the Catholic Church, excommunicated. He did not leave it of his own accord.

In all of this, I hope that Luther's stress on the Holy Spirit is clear. Again, it is a mediating position. Neither is the Spirit a matter of secondary importance as has been true historically within Catholicism, nor is it, on the other hand, the dramatically personal kind of experience, manifest in the speaking in tongues, or glossolalia, so characteristic of the Pentecostal wing of the church. The Spirit is instead the continuing power of God, who supports the individual member of the church in *all* his activities, producing *all* things. The Spirit does not make himself manifest merely in glossolalia but in prayer, in love, in patience and kindness and faith—these things are the fruits of the Spirit. All of them are the accomplishments of the Spirit, who calls us each one and equips each one to live out his peculiar and unique vocation within the church.

Which of these three views is closest to the truth, more valid or pertinent than the others? As well ask which blade of a pair of scissors is the more important! All views are valid. All are necessary. Any one view without the others is but a partial truth, and a half-truth is always half a lie. Luther and Calvin, by themselves, taken in sterile isolation, could produce a passivity that borders on quietism and even fatalism. If man is but to submit passively to a divine work upon himself, the result can be a loss of all sense of individual and social responsibility. The view that all men are called of God, the concept of vocation, can likewise be abused, and can lead to an impoverishment of the church. If a man can serve God as well as a businessman, making $47,500.13 a year, as he can as a country parson, making one tenth that sum, why go into the ministry at all? The Lutheran-Calvinistic view of vocation, driven to an extreme, can lead to a church without a head, a deformed monster, a people without a pastor, a populace deprived of prophetic leadership.

The Catholic view, taken by itself, can degenerate, as we have already said, into a religious club. In the old Israel, sacrifices for sin as guilt produced a dead people, going through the rituals of sacrifice, buying God off for another year by giving him four quarts of bull blood at an annual feast. When that sorry day was arrived at, prophets like Isaiah and Amos rose up to denounce the whole sacrificial system, and Jesus himself went through the Temple, driving out the priests with a whip.

The Pentecostal view, in rigid lonely isolation, is equally open to abuse. What begins as a plea for man to shoulder responsibility and stand accountable before God can lead to baptized humanism. The stress on man's response, taken by itself, can produce a generation of activists working out their own salvation through their own efforts. Legalism has always been the burden of this element. Further, the left wing of Protestantism has always been peculiarly exposed to the excesses of the social gospel, the naïve and always failing belief that man can through his own efforts and resolve transform society and produce Utopia in our day and in our time.

Each of these three emphases has something to tell us, something that we need. The history of Christendom is astounding proof that God's will, even despite men if not through them, will be done. Whenever one emphasis or aspect of the paradoxical truth of Christianity was lost or neglected within the church, a new sect, a new denomination, would arise, making that neglected idea its central tenet. When the church stumbled into the error of looking upon this life as the whole show, stressing man's role here and now at the expense of a hope of heaven later on, apocalyptic or eschatological or Adventist groups came into being, stressing the imminent return of Christ and the life of the world to come. When the Lutheran Reformation began to degenerate and drove Luther's ideas of "Faith Alone" to such an extreme that all emphasis on good works and personal piety was inundated by a preoccupation with sterile theology, the German Pietistic movement came into being stressing the necessity of personal commitment. When the church became one-sided in its emphasis on the divinity of Jesus, ignoring his true humanity, sects such as the Jehovah's Witnesses came into being, stressing the other extreme, arguing for the humanity, and the humanity alone, of Jesus. The paradoxical many-splendored grandeur of Christian teaching, which includes many contradictory but nonetheless vital emphases, seems to be too large a bundle for any one generation or denomination to hold all by itself. The whole truth is heard only by listening to these many voices being raised together, sorting out their excesses, and balancing their insights together with the equally important insights of the other denominations.

This is not to plead for relativism, to argue for the absurd belief that it does not make any difference what you believe as long as you truly believe it. If nothing else, Christianity argues for an *absolute,* for the conviction that there is an ultimate reality that exists quite independently of how we may conceive of it. Man is not the measure of all things. Rather, I am arguing that Christian truth, an *absolute,* can be seen from a variety of perspectives, all of them valid. It is like a house around which we walk, looking in the windows. Which window you look into will determine just how you see the interior. Your perspectives will be different, but the ultimate reality remains the same. We are not saved by our theology. Theology is a man-made scaffolding, the product of history and circumstance. We are saved instead by God in Jesus Christ, the absolute to whom our theologies point and bear witness.

Chapter Five

ESCHATOLOGY

THIS chapter title, "Eschatology," comes from two Greek words, one of which we have already looked at. In the Introduction we noted that "ology" comes from *logia,* meaning "a word about" or "a study of." Everybody knows "ology" in such words as psychology, a word about the psyche or mind, or sociology, a study of society. The other Greek word, *eschatos,* is not so well known. It is a peculiarly Biblical word, and outside the circles of serious Biblical study it is practically unknown. *Eschatos* means "last" or "final." Thus eschatology is a study of or a word about the last or final things. The word sums up the conviction of the earliest church that the world was hastening to its end, that the goal and consummation of all human history was upon them; they were, they thought, living in the final hours of the world clock.

To understand in full the breadth and depth of this idea, we have to return to some of the ideas we looked at in Chapter Three, especially when we were discussing Gustaf Aulén's "classic" theory of the atonement. First of all, Aulén called it the *"classic"* theory because it went back to the classical age of the church; it was the conviction of the *earliest* church. Aulén insisted that the "moral renewal" theory and the "satisfaction" theory had arrived much later on the field. It was the "classic" theory which dominated the earliest church's view. Secondly, Aulén insisted that this theory could also be called the *Christus Victor* theory. That is, the earliest view of the church saw Jesus as a conquerer, as a triumphant warrior come to do battle with the devil.

There really can be little doubt that Aulén is correct. This *was* the view of the earliest church. Mark, the first Gospel written, concentrates most of all on the miracle stories. Over

60 percent of this first Gospel deals, directly or indirectly, with miracles—miracles showing Jesus lashing out at all the manifestations of the devil's power. The people believed that hunger was demonic, and Jesus fed the multitudes. But most of all, the devil ruled through death, and Jesus both raised the dead and himself arose from the dead. The apostle Paul too, like Mark, conceived of Jesus' work within this context of conflict, and the words that he used primarily to describe the work of Jesus were not the words of the "moral renewal" or "satisfaction" theories, such as "reconciliation," or "forgiveness," or "repentance," but rather words from the *Christus Victor* theory, such as "liberation," "salvation," "redemption," etc.

All this is background for the proper comprehension of the word "eschatology." It appears that this battle with the devil was marked by two major campaigns: the resurrection of Jesus and the return of Jesus at the end of human history. The resurrection of Jesus was that critical moment when he established his superiority over the devil, when he proved by the empty tomb that he was stronger than the evil one. We have already seen how this stress on the resurrection was the beating heart of the earliest Christian proclamation. But this resurrection was not the end of Satan's power. It was instead the assurance that Satan's power would end, that he had met his match in Jesus, that he had used his most powerful weapon —the tomb—and it was powerless to hold the divine Warrior. The resurrection was not the end of the cosmic war, the final destruction of Satan. Rather, it was the turning point in that war, the indication of who was the stronger of the combatants.

Every war has a turning point, a point at which, even though the war continues, it is already clear who will eventually win. For example, most military observers are convinced that the critical turning point in World War II, the point at which the outcome was put beyond all doubt, was the Battle of the Bulge in December, 1944. The Allied forces had streamed across France and had driven toward the German border, a long thin line aiming at the heartland of Germany. Hitler gathered together all his panzer divisions, the bulk of his tanks, and massed them north of this Allied line of advance in Belgium. Then, in the offensive now known as the Battle of the Bulge, he smashed to the south. It was a tactic as old as the Romans, *divide et impera,* divide and rule. If he could have split the Allied forces, he could have turned eastward and mopped up the troops cut off, and then turned westward to try to drive the main body back into France. The Allied line bulged and sagged to the south, hence the name of the battle, but did not break. Hitler's last desperate gamble was lost, and so was the war. The last German heavy equipment was destroyed. The turning point had occurred. From this moment on, the end of the war was no longer in question. The Allies would win. But even though victory was assured, the war dragged on for many months. Soldiers on both sides still lost their lives, even though an Allied victory was inevitable.

In somewhat the same way the earliest church understood the relationship between Jesus' resurrection and his return (the Biblical word to describe Jesus' return is "parousia," a word referring to the enthronement of a king, to his appearance in glory). Jesus' resurrection was the turning point, the establishment of his superiority, the act or victory that put the eventual end beyond all doubt. And the Parousia would be the actual end of the war, the moment when he returned, destroying fully and finally the forces of the devil. The war went on, but the church believed itself to be on the winning side. It is this conviction which lies behind the otherwise incomprehensible language of Paul. Running throughout his letters is the paradoxical combination of great suffering and great joy. For example, in I Thess. 1:6 he reminds the Thessalonians that they have received the word of Jesus in "much affliction, with joy." They were afflicted, suffered much, because the enemy was still active, attacking them, directing at them the wrath aimed earlier at Jesus. They received it "in much joy" because even as they suffered they were convinced that they were on the winning side and the end was in sight.

This same combination of joy and suffering runs all through Paul's letters. For example, in Rom., ch. 8, Paul in one place can list the catalog of agonies to which the church is exposed as the demonic host seeks to wreak havoc on them. In vs. 35–39 of that chapter he speaks of tribulation, distress, persecution, famine, nakedness, the sword—all the weapons that the "principalities and powers" (his words for the Satanic heavenly host) heap on the church. Yet he can face that somber list of weapons with the exultant shout of eventual victory, the insistence that nothing "in all creation will be able to separate us from the love of God in Christ Jesus our Lord." Even earlier than that, in the same chapter, v. 18, he can insist that the sufferings of the present hour simply are not worth fretting over or being troubled about in the light of the impending victory, the coming moment when the whole creation will be made new, and the cosmos itself "set free from its bondage" (see especially v. 21).

This conviction that the turning point was past and the ultimate victory imminent also accounts for the flaming hope for the soon-to-arrive end of the world that characterized the earliest Christians. It accounts for their eschatology. They saw the end of the world, not as a moment of judgment to be feared, but as a moment of liberation, the time of freedom, the glorious future when the divided, afflicted, present existence, lived out simultaneously under Satan and the Spirit, would end and God alone would rule. They did not fear the end but yearned for it with every fiber of their existence. The present world was an evil age, overrun by demonic powers, but the turning point was past and Christ was coming soon!

This conviction that Christ was coming soon as the divine liberator dominates all the earliest New Testament books. Jesus, even though he confesses in Mark 13:32 that—as a human being, a true man with limited knowledge—he does not know exactly when that end will come, seems to insist nonetheless that it will come in the lifetime of those who heard him. In Mark 9:1 he tells his disciples that not all of them will die "before they see the kingdom of God come with power." In Mark 14:62, at his trial, Jesus tells the high priest that he will be alive to see the Son of Man coming in power on the clouds of heaven bringing all of human history to a close. The apostle Paul, in I Thess. 4:15, 17, reflects the same conviction, insisting that he himself will be alive when Jesus returns. He speaks of "*we* who are left . . . *we* who are alive" at the return of Jesus, numbering himself with those who will survive to see Jesus' Parousia. Thus, the earliest church, patterning itself after Jesus' own words, warmly looked forward in ardent hope to the final hour. They believed that the interval between resurrection and return would be a brief one—extended only long enough for Jesus to mount up to heaven and assemble the divine troops of God, the angels, and then return in final, fiery glory to destroy the devil and all his works and all his ways.

But the end never came. The delay of the Parousia was the profoundest, the most troublesome problem the earliest church faced. How explain this apparent failure of Jesus to bring the cosmic war to a close? Even in Paul's day this lengthening of the interval was a burning problem. Paul's answer to the dilemma was to insist that the interval had a positive purpose: in that pause the word might be preached and the elect of God assembled. But Paul's answer eventually proved inadequate as the interval continued to extend itself. Some new answer had to be given. Why had Christ not returned? Why had the Kingdom not come?

There were really only two routes open to the church, either the route of despair or the avenue of transmuted and transformed expectations. Either they could say that Jesus had not returned because he *could not* return, that Satan, who was stronger than earlier believed, was able to resist and hold back the advancing armies of God, and that the world was forever doomed to live out its days under his malignant power. Or else they could say that the whole structure of Christian thought could be reexamined and reformed and it could be argued that the Kingdom *had come* in an unexpected and earlier unseen way.

This second route was the way taken by the church. In an agonizing and far-reaching restructuring of its entire basic thought, the church came to the conclusion that the rule of God *had* come. Jesus was already in charge, in full charge, of the present scene. Demonic resistance had already been ended, in the past, in the lifetime of Jesus himself. The Fourth Gospel, John, written very late (probably about the year A.D. 100, a full seventy years after the resurrection, when the failure of the Parousia could no longer be ignored or easily explained away), develops this new and altered conviction. For example, John 12:31 and 16:11 both speak of Satan as the ruler or prince of this world, but both verses go on to insist that this ruler, in the past tense, has *already* been thrown down, defeated. In the same manner, John 3:18 speaks of men being *already* condemned or *already* saved, right then in the present hour, not waiting for salvation sometime far off in the future. This is called *realized* eschatology, eschatology already accomplished. The Kingdom, the rule of God, is *now*, not in the future alone. The world had already been liberated and restored to God's rule.

This is the way the delay of the return of Jesus came to be explained, the *only* way it *could be* explained without giving up the conviction that Jesus was victorious. Since his victory, his Parousia, the end of the war, had never come, one had to say either that it would not come, that he had failed, or else that he had already won the war. The church took the latter view.

It was this conviction which opened the door to the loss of the "classic" theory and its eventual replacement by the "moral renewal" and "satisfaction" theories. Since it was now felt that Satan had already been beaten, it could no longer be seriously argued that sin was bondage. How could man be in bondage to a beaten foe? Sin could only be seen as an act of responsible man—rebellion—or as the consequence of that act of responsible man—guilt. It was not just the view of sin and of man that underwent a change, man now being seen as free and not in servitude, sin being seen as act rather than condition. The whole spectrum of early Christian theology had to be reformed. No longer, for example, could suffering be seen as an attack by Satan. It had to be seen as a punishment of God instead. Hebrews 12:7–11 develops this later point of view. In direct opposition to Luke 13:16, where Jesus saw the suffering of the crippled woman as due to Satanic attack, this Hebrews passage insists that suffering originates in God. It is purgative or cleansing in purpose, designed to correct and chastise the wayward, charged with positive purpose, in much the same way that a concerned father disciplines his children.

The world was no longer viewed as the demonic playground where Satan's arbitrary caprice was made manifest in random attacks on the elect. Instead, the world was seen as a good place under God's rule, a place where all that unrolled was due to his divine will.

It was this new conviction which paved the way for the later view of Tertullian that sin was guilt and suffering divinely instituted cleansing. Some way had to be found to explain the abundance of agony the church was undergoing in the persecutions it faced under the Romans. When Jesus did not return, it was despair to say that the suffering was Satanic in origin, for that would indicate that all was lost. Instead, the church looked on these things as the will of God, acts designed to cleanse the church through discipline.

The whole concept of God or of Christ was destined to change. Jesus came to be no longer looked upon as the divine liberator who was in the future to destroy the devil and set man free. The devil had already been thrown down; man was already set free. Thus Jesus was not seen as a divine and future deliverer, but rather as a present judge, meting out the just punishments for sin on the people of God, making them pure. Jesus the liberator was replaced by Jesus the judge, even as sin as bondage was replaced by sin as guilt. It is this new view of Jesus and of sin which paved the way for the eventual medieval concepts of the intercession of the saints and the pleas addressed to Mary, Jesus' mother. Sin was guilt, guilt that had to be punished. The scales had to be balanced before one could enter into heaven. Those whose bad acts outweighed their good acts would either have to suffer here or in purgatory.

But there were those whose good acts did, in fact, outweigh their venial or bad acts. They had a surplus of merit in their favor. They went straight to heaven without going to purgatory. That is what a saint is according to ancient Catholic conviction, one whose ledger showed a credit balance, a surplus of good deeds. But, in medieval Christian thought, that surplus could be used! Even as Jesus' merits, earned through his vicarious death on the cross, could be used to blot out original guilt, so also the excess merits of the saints could be used to offset actual guilt. One could borrow from their surplus to offset one's own deficit. The whole structure of prayers to the saints thus arose. The adulation of Mary, the appeal to the mother of Jesus, is but a part of this structure of thought. The veneration of the saints, so typical of the church for centuries, was inevitable once it became clear that Jesus was not returning soon and that sin had to be seen in some way other than as bondage to Satan. Once the Parousia was delayed, it was inevitable that the *Christus Victor* theory would be replaced by the "satisfaction" or "penal" theory.

Before going any farther, we must make the same point we made earlier, namely, that the emergence of these new views does not represent a negation or a contradiction of the earlier views as much as a complement or needed addition to those earlier views. It is not an either/or but a both/and. Notice well, we now have *two* views of suffering—as the work of Satan and as the will of God. We have two concepts of the Kingdom of God—as a present reality and as a future hope. Both of these are true. There is a sense in which suffering is undeserved, a miscarriage of justice. Who can look at a maimed infant, a senseless catastrophe of nature, a malignant disease falling upon the innocent as well as upon the guilty, without coming to realize that there is a dimension of absurdity and caprice in the world in which we live? It simply is not true that the righteous always prosper and the evil fall. "Crime does not pay" makes a nice cliché to bolster law enforcement officials' morale in their work, but it *is* a cliché, and there are so many exceptions, so many cases where crime *has* paid (it is said that half the real estate in Miami Beach is owned by the sons of the mobsters who worked with Al Capone), that the proposition cannot be seriously defended.

But, on the other hand, there is a moral streak in the world in which we live, running right alongside the amoral or immoral. There is a sense in which we reap what we sow, and our wrong deeds bring disaster and despair upon us. The man who abuses his body or despises his loved ones wrecks his body and alienates his loved ones. The man who cheats in marriage ultimately cheats not God (God is going to be holy whether or not that man carries on illicitly) or his mate but himself. He deprives himself of ever fully understanding the intimacy and the joy to be found in unselfish self-giving. *Both* are true. It is not an either/or.

And the same thing is true with the Christian concept of the Kingdom as both future and present. When either of these emphases is lost, distortion enters in. When the emphasis falls solely and exclusively on the future, on salvation as something out there, this present world loses all significance, becomes irrelevant, and all efforts to improve or alter conditions cease. Karl Marx was right, or at least partially right, when he said that religion is an opiate of the people. It *can* be an opiate, a drug, rendering man unconscious, making him docile and willing to accept any and all abuse heaped on him here and now. Make man think of heaven and look for recompense there, and you can stick him into a sweatshop here and now, grind the life out of him, and make him work eighty hours a week for an inadequate salary. Promise him heaven and do what you will with him on earth. The future look, pure and alone, can be the most world-denying, suffocating form of organized religious tyranny, opening the door to hideous abuse and tragic resignation.

On the other hand, when this world is seen as the full story, and the future hope is lost, again something significant falls out of the picture. Religion is replaced by ethical activism, and the social do-gooders take over with their one-dimensional programs, seeking to reform all society, to create heaven here and now. On the one hand, this reduces man to an apple core, an animal, a vegetable, denying that he has any eternal life or enduring dignity beyond his threescore and ten years. On the other hand, this social activism always and inevitably leads to despair because we never do and never can arrive at Utopia here and now. The old Y.M.C.A. morality—transform society and we will produce heaven on earth, build enough swimming pools and get rid of sin in our day—has failed and will always fail. The poor are always with us. We build a shiny recreation center, and the kids walk out and on the way home kick in all the windows of the church. We can change man's environment but we do not make man better. Our technological advance has far outstripped the myth of man's moral progress, and our very advances threaten to destroy us.

Both of these emphases—the world as good, the world as evil; the Kingdom as present, the Kingdom as future—are mutually self-supporting, and not contradictory. The whole Christian truth is not known until they are taken together in tension and held simultaneously. We *do* believe that this is God's good world, and thus to be improved and worked on. Our best efforts are demanded in seeking to ameliorate suffering and improve environment. The church *does* concern itself with social issues, with humanitarian programs, because God *is* concerned with and involved in what happens here and now. But we also recognize that there is more to life than threescore and ten, that man is more than a fleeting spot on the passing scene. He has an eternal destiny, a God-ordained enduring worth that does not end when this day's work is over. Either emphasis without the other is incomplete.

To return to the question of eschatology, we have seen how the delay in the end of the world reshaped and altered Christian expectation. Other things, other historical factors, have also had their effect as we have moved down the long corridor of centuries, producing in their turn altered emphases within Christian theology.

Probably the two most formative factors in the shaping of contemporary theology have been the Renaissance, on the one hand, and the rise of scientific or technological advance, on the other. These two are not, of course, separate, but we will try nonetheless to treat them separately. We cannot treat them in full, but some general observations can and must be made if we are to understand where the church is today and why it is there.

The Renaissance means exactly what that French word says, "a rebirth," a rebirth of the ancient Hellenistic conviction that man was a giant, able to mold and model his own destiny. Even as Alexander wanted to make the deserts bloom, convinced that man had locked up in his own head the key to all his problems, so also the Renaissance shared that conviction. It was the view that man was a giant, awakening, coming out into the light of a new day, emerging from the Dark Ages. This belief in the power and the size of man shows up in all the Renaissance and post-Renaissance art and literature and philosophy. Michelangelo, for example, was a Christian. But he was a Christian *humanist* as well, convinced and convicted of the power of man. When he painted God on the roof of the Sistine chapel, he painted Adam right next to God, and Adam was every bit as big as God! Rabelais' Gargantua was a stumbling, bumbling giant, causing havoc on every side—but he *was* a giant coming into his own! Swift's Gulliver was a giant, living among the midget Lilliputians. All these works of art and literature converge on the one central conviction—that man is enormous in size, a giant with fantastic power and potential.

This emerging confidence, this rebirth of optimistic belief in the power of man, did not crowd Christianity off the scene so much as it altered Christianity. Jesus, for example, came to be seen no longer as divine liberator (man could deliver himself), or even as judge. Rather, as Renaissance convictions rooted and flowered, Jesus came to be thought first and foremost as a human model, an exemplar, a type after which powerful emergent man was to pattern himself. The human side of Jesus came to be stressed in theological circles, as men sought to strip off the incrustations and superstitions of a bygone age which had wrongly, it was believed, stressed the divine side of Jesus, and to lay bare the true human portrait of Jesus so that the model could stand forth sharp and clear and strong.

Albert Schweitzer, for example, wrote a book at the turn of this century entitled *The Quest of the Historical Jesus,* and what this book reveals more than anything else is the total absorption of the theologians of the nineteenth century with the quest for the truly human Jesus. Many other factors play into this writing by Schweitzer, but the point we stress here is simply that his book summarizes and symbolizes this new attitude toward Jesus, this new understanding of man. The first three quarters of the book is a review of the views of the scholars of the preceding generation. Schweitzer parades them all past us, showing how each one of them was concerned to lay bare the truly human Jesus, the truly human Jesus set free from the supernatural trappings heaped on him by the earlier church. The miracles are systematically set aside. Did Jesus walk on the water? Not really. He was standing on a log floating just below the surface, or he was standing on a submerged sandbar, and the disciples simply did not realize how close to the shore they had rowed. Did Jesus really feed the multitudes? Not exactly. What he did was to open his sandwich bag and give something to eat to a man in the front row. Another man saw this example of selflessness and, inspired, did likewise. Soon the entire crowd was enjoying lunch.

The miracles were discounted and denied not simply because of a bias against miracles per se, but rather because the attempt was being made to cast Jesus as a true human being, and only a true human being—a model that man could follow. Man is a giant, responsible and free, endowed with great potential. What he needs is a model, not a savior sprinkling bread crumbs on him. It was believed that by ripping off all the theological platitudes and creations of a past superstitious age that model could be found in Jesus. This emphasis on man as a giant is the heritage of the Renaissance and its effect was a new understanding of Jesus neither as liberator nor as judge but as exemplar, worthy model for worthy man.

At this point the second emphasis comes in and blends with the Renaissance—the rise of technology, the scientific explosion. One should begin, not with the natural sciences—physics, chemistry, etc.—but rather with the biological sciences. One should begin with Darwin. Charles Darwin's book *On the Origin of Species* was probably the most revolutionary and formative book of the last two centuries. It was revolutionary but not in the way most men see it. The church was, of course, alarmed and disturbed when the study appeared. The "science" of the Bible seemed to be contradicted. Darwin argued, in effect, that the world did not come into being in seven short days, approximately four thousand years before Jesus was born, with man being made in an immediate way by the direct intervention of God. Rather, the world was thousands and thousands, even millions and millions, of years old. Creation did not take place in seven days but in endless aeons. Man was not made immediately but was produced mediately, evolving over millions of years out of an insignificant amoeba, passing eventually into ape form, and then slowly coming forth first as Neanderthal man and only lastly as man as we know him.

This apparent contradiction of the Bible's "science" rocked the church. Enormous controversies developed which at first tried to refute evolution as a theory, later becoming more sophisticated and trying not to refute but rather to harmonize science with religion. For example, the "days" of the Old Testament Creation story were looked at anew and came to be reinterpreted, being described not as twenty-four-hour periods but rather as roughly corresponding to the endless aeons of the evolutionary theory. Without going into all the details, while some theologians continue even now to try to refute science or harmonize the Biblical Creation story with science, it is true to say that in the main the problem has come to be seen as academic and irrelevant. Most theologians and scientists are ready and willing to agree that the two accounts are not so much in conflict as they are concerned about different things. Science is concerned with the "How?" Religion is concerned with the "Why?" The Bible is taken, usually, as a poetic or theological account of *who* created man and *why* man was created and *where* he is going. He is a creature under God, and whether he came into being immediately (as Genesis seems to say in its poetic language) or whether he came into being mediately (as Darwin says), the issue is not basically a conflict, for science deals with a process whereas theology deals with a purpose. With that the issue seemed to be solved or at least an uneasy truce arranged.

But as I said, the real threat of Darwinism (if "threat" is the proper word) comes in a quite different area. Darwinism as a biological theory is no problem, but Darwinism soon ceased to be pure biology and came to be philosophy. A new view of man arose, a view not entirely new but which carried the earlier insight and conviction of the Renaissance even farther.

The enormous impact of Darwinism was in its understanding of man. Man was not, according to this theory, first good and only later evil. He was not made perfect and flawless only to fall later into bondage to sin. Instead, he had begun on his belly in the slime of the jungle, and every day in every way— slowly but surely—he was getting better all the time! He began as an amoeba in a primeval swamp, had become an ape and then a man, and the end was still not in sight! The overwhelming conviction of man's great potential became an axiom of the day. An exultant optimism arose. Give man enough time and even as he had licked the jungle and ceased being a monkey, so also in time he would cease being a fool. In time he would lick the slums, the labor problems, and every other problem in the world. Now "Invictus" could be written: "I am the master of my fate; I am the captain of my soul." Here is where the challenge, unseen in most places, was laid down to the church. Man was not a sinner, by nature sinful and unclean. He was instead an emerging giant whose problems could all be answered and mastered by education and proper example. The earlier beliefs of man as a victim under Satan could now be set aside as irrelevant superstitious vestiges of a credulous ignorant age. Man needed no savior other than his own insight and effort.

This buoyant enthusiasm was fed by extraordinary accomplishments produced by technological advance. As education advanced, the areas earlier staked out by religion as its own peculiar preserve were shrunken. There was a time when the savage prowling the green floor of the primeval jungle would hear the thunder and see the lightning above and, unable to explain these things in any other way, would attribute the phenomena to the activities of the gods. This province of religion was invaded; God was shrunken. Today we have weather maps, cold fronts, low-pressure areas, meteorological satellites, and other equipment that can measure weather, and all these things have made lightning and thunder no longer a religious problem, no longer celestial spares and strikes, but rather a scientific study.

There was a time when, if a loved one fell ill, the disease was seen in theological terms. One could say, with Luke 13:16, that Satan was attacking and causing pain. Or one could say, with Heb. 12:7, that God was punishing as a disciplining father would. In either case it was a theological problem. Today, however, in the days of Dr. Barnard of Africa and Dr. Cooley of Texas, medicine is no longer a theological problem but a scientific problem. Who, today, having a toothache, cries out that Satan is stabbing him in the molars? We get a headache and we go not to the pastor for prayer but to the pharmacist for aspirin. If a loved one gets cancer, it is not to the church that we fly but rather to the finest surgeon money can obtain and to cobalt and radium treatments. God has shrunk in size. Technological advance, with all its already accomplished miracles, is the real hope and answer to man's dilemma. True, many problems yet remain, but man has already conquered many and will, given time, conquer the rest as well.

There was a time, in the Old Testament, when enemy invasion from abroad or economic collapse from within were seen as signs of God's displeasure, a punishment inflicted on a wayward people. Today we have the United Nations on one hand and the Keynesian theory of economics on the other. The United Nations is a feeble and trembling thing not yet producing on its great potential, but it does have potential in the eyes of many; it is the hope of the world, the forum where we can come and reason together, the only potential answer to the resolving of the world's conflicts. We need no longer fear depression, for we have learned, thanks to Lord Keynes, how to control the economy through raising and lowering taxes, and the Great Society, its creation and sharing, is the hope of our day. God has shrunk, squeezed off the scene by emergent man's massive, mighty accomplishments.

This translation of Darwinism from a biological theory into a philosophical conception of man as an emerging giant has produced two theological movements in our day, one popular and the other more scholarly or theological.

The popular one is perhaps best summarized by the recent "death of God" furor. That movement is in one sense already dead. Theology, like ladies' hats, has its fads, and the "death of God" movement was in one sense only a passing fad, exploding on all the covers of the national magazines and then fading equally rapidly into oblivion. But in another sense it was no fad at all; it was instead the inevitable result of those emphases which we have been examining. It was the direct outgrowth of the conviction that man was a giant and getting better, that progress was inevitable. If you really want to understand the movement, then throw away the slogan "God is dead" and substitute for it the phrase "Man is alive"! That is what the movement sought to say. The advocates of the theory point to all the things we have just looked at, technological advances in medicine, in weather, in how to control wars and govern an economy. All these advances prove that man can, given enough time, improve his environment and conquer his ills.

Why cower in a cathedral on your knees praying to some celestial specter in the skies? All you will do in that posture is wear out the knees of your trousers. Kneeling in prayer for your hungry neighbor down the street will not cause it to rain turkeys on his front porch. Instead, roll up your sleeves, go to work, tackle your problems, live like a man, a mighty man with great potential; don't live like a frightened rabbit behind stained-glass windows. This is the heart and thrust of the "God is dead" movement, and though the movement itself fades away, the impulses that produced it are vitally alive, throbbing throughout our society, for the conviction of the greatness of man is upon us on all sides. It can be seen that intimately embedded in this movement is a denial of transcendentalism, a rejection of the belief in a transcendent or celestial supernatural power outside man, controlling or shaping his life and way. Man is not open to the interference of supernatural powers, good or bad, Holy Spirit or evil spirit. Man is instead himself responsible for what befalls him. And in the "God is dead" movement Jesus survives, if he survives at all, solely as a human model, an example for man to follow in his quest for improvement and eventual perfection.

The scholarly approach to the problem, though presented in different language and apparently aimed at slightly different problems, proceeds with the same assumptions and works toward the same answer. This scholarly approach is called "demythologizing," and its leading advocate is the German theologian Rudolf Bultmann. Although an old man now and retired, Bultmann for many years served as professor of New Testament at Marburg University in Germany. He was also a perceptive and powerful man, and his writings have helped shape current theological views probably more than the writings of any other twentieth-century theologian. Bultmann's main thesis runs in several broad points. First of all, he concedes without any argument whatever that the basic thrust of the Biblical message concentrates on the belief in the reality of demonic powers and the belief in an impending end of the world. He approves and affirms all that we have already seen and said about Jesus' work being a struggle with the devil that would result in the close of the age. This was basic, he insists, to the thought of Jesus. Bultmann begins a two-volume study of the thought of the New Testament by insisting that the whole structure of Jesus' thought revolved around and was built upon the twin emphases of demonology and eschatology. Jesus believed that the present world was corrupted by Satan and ruled by him. But Jesus saw his own life as a struggle against that foe, a struggle that he would win, closing out this present evil age and ushering in the eschatologocal Kingdom of God.

That is point one of Bultmann's program, the honest, ruthlessly honest and insistent argument that, whether we like it or not, those are the categories which determined Jesus' own comprehension of his work. Bultmann at this point represents a refreshing breath of fresh air wafting through theological circles. For years, even for centuries, the church has been embarrassed by these motifs of demonology and eschatology and has either soft-pedaled, minimized, or even ignored and denied those ideas, pretending that they were not there, seeking to make something more "spiritual" out of the mesage of Jesus. Those ideas troubled us, seemed to smack of a naïve prescientific cosmology when men foolishly believed that the world was flat and the cosmos was a three-storied structure, with God up in heaven, the devil in the basement, and man caught between heaven and hell. Embarrassed by this antiquated terminology, the church pretended or claimed that it was not there. Enough of this playing of word games, argues Bultmann. Those thoughts *are* there, and they are basic to Jesus and the primitive church.

But, and this is point two of Bultmann's argument, those ideas, so dear to Jesus and those of his day in the earliest church, simply do not make sense in our own scientific day. Who among us, he asks, can turn on the radio, use a telephone, buy a television set, go to the doctor for a penicillin injection when we have an infection, and continue to maintain that the world is a playground for little green imps? Who can take demonology seriously today, arguing for Satan as controlling our psyche, when modern psychology and psychiatry have made their enormous contributions, showing us that man is not the result of divine interference, beneficial or malignant, but is instead a responsible creature impinged upon, but not determined by, environment and heredity? Who can continue to take eschatology seriously now that two thousand years have rolled by since the original announcement was made that the end was in sight?

To continue to insist on these antiquated ideas is to reduce the church to the charge of obscurantism and to alienate it from the world. To continue to preach that now outdated message is to drive away the very people we seek to reach, and it is to be dishonest in that very process. It is dishonest because even the most radical Bible-pounding fundamentalist who continues to argue for the validity of those ideas really does not believe in them! One can say all one wants to say, Bultmann notes, about agreeing with Jesus that Satan causes sickness, but where does the fundamentalist go when he is ill? To the altar or to the aspirin bottle? The answer is both obvious and profoundly significant. By going to trained medical specialists one is making clear his own deepest conviction that no matter what he says in the abstract he really sees suffering not as a theological issue but as a technological or medical problem. Or one can repeat every Sunday morning in the words of the Apostles' Creed one's conviction that Jesus will return at the end of time. But who, having confessed it, believes it? *Really* believes it? Which Bible-pounding fundamentalist, when he wakes up in the morning, is surprised that he woke up in the morning? Was he *really* looking for the end of the world? Why, then, does he subscribe to a retirement and pension plan? As he strolls across the parking lot of the church on the way to Sunday services, on his way to a recitation of eschatological expectations in the uttering of the Apostles' Creed, is he looking up at the heavens waiting for Jesus to pop through the clouds surrounded by angels tootling on trumpets bringing all human history to a close? The very ludicrousness of the questions serve as their answers. Modern man, who cut his teeth on the scientific view, simply will not accept that medieval point of view, and to seek to thrust it on him is to thrust him away.

That, then, is point two of Bultmann's program: to recognize that even though Jesus and the early church believed in those categories of thought, modern man does not and will not.

Point three grows out of this. If the church is to survive and continue, those ancient concepts must be rewritten and reinterpreted, put into a new and contemporary language that speaks significantly to the altered social and cultural scene. The older bizarre imagery must be stripped away and replaced by new imagery that makes sense in our time. The poetic myths of the Biblical language must be discarded. That is the source of the word "demythologizing." What must be done is that the *form* of the original message must be altered—not the *content,* just the *form.* A new expression of the ancient truths must be hammered out. A new vocabulary must be achieved. Take the ancient idea of demonology. Take it and retain it, but do not speak in terms of Satan and the demons. Instead, use the language of psychology that lies ready at hand. Speak of the id, the libido, the Oedipus complex, of a compulsive delinquent, or of any of the other terms. Speak of man as exposed to harmful forces, but make those forces part of his own psychic composition, using the language of the social sciences instead of making those forces into cosmic entities, evil independent personalities that exist in their own right. Make that change and *then* modern man will better be able to grasp what the original message of Jesus can mean to him today. Or, with eschatology, continue to talk about it, about the end of the age, but do not talk of it as a historical event lying out in some as yet unfulfilled future. Instead, talk about it in personal or existential terms. There is a critical moment when every man stands before God, alone, judged, and called to account. It is a moment when all eternity is held in the balance. But that critical moment is not future, when half-dressed angels blare away on divine trumpets on the lip of eternity ushering in the final age. Rather, that moment is now, when man stands confronted by Jesus, by the demand for decision. Right here, right now, as I make my stand as a responsible person for or against Jesus—*that* is the critical moment of my life when I pass from death unto life. Speak of eschatology in *those* terms, in existential terms or in personal terms, but not in historical or cosmological language, and then modern man can comprehend and appreciate the meaning of Jesus' message for our day.

Different as this may be in one sense from the popular "God is dead" movement, it can be seen how this scholarly approach really deals with the same set of facts and works with the same presuppositions. Both views are powerfully influenced by modern technological advance which seems to render obsolete much of the older Biblical message. And both points of view are based on the optimistic, affirmative view of man as a giant, able through his own strength to solve his own problems—neither interfered with by Satan nor helped by good celestial forces moving man along like some pawn in celestial chess. Both points of view are one in accepting the advances of science as indicative of man's great potential, his inevitable progress. In both cases, Jesus is not so much Savior as example.

This point of view, this unbounded optimism in man's capacity, has produced a reaction. On the one hand, there was the powerful commentary on Romans, written by Karl Barth, which appeared right after World War I. That book was, in effect, a strong protest against this optimistic view of man. Man, mighty man, who was making such spectacular progress leaping from pinnacle to pinnacle, had gone back into the trenches of war like an insane, enraged animal! This was the "inconceivable war," as Barth called it. Inconceivable! How could man, if he *was* that mighty and making such progress, revert to the role of a savage? The conviction that progress was automatic and that man was ascending ever upward, able of his own reason and strength to produce perfection, was dealt a staggering blow in the eyes of Barth. And this staggering blow has been followed up by others which seem to be able to shatter this buoyant enthusiasm.

World War I was followed by the American depression, which in turn was followed by World War II, which was followed by the Korean conflict, and in the midst of all that "progress" there came first the atom bomb and then the hydro-

gen bomb, arms so devastatingly destructive that human existence itself now seems threatened. No longer is the threat of
the end of all human life to be seen simply as a religious exag-
geration, a relic of a superstitious bygone age, but it was and
is now a possibility, an awesome possibility. The mighty man
of the turn of the century has for a son one who was born in a
World War and matured in a depression, and for a grandson
one who may die, face down, in a rice paddy in Vietnam.
Where is this enormous progress so hymned by the liberal
movement?

Certainly this unbridled enthusiasm of the Bultmanns and
the "God is dead" theologians is not shared by the poets and
playwrights of our day. Arthur Miller writes, in *Death of a
Salesman*, of a poor little man who never knew who he was.
Jean-Paul Sartre and Albert Camus have won Nobel prizes for
literature with their depiction of an absurd world lacking in
purpose or plan, a world in which man must simply grit his
teeth in the face of the absurdity of death. J. D. Salinger, in his
book which was the Bible of the youth of a decade ago,
Catcher in the Rye, shows a confused young Holden Caulfield
looking for answers, desperately searching, turning at last in
his final hour to the one man who had given him a vision, a
hope, a sense of direction—his English teacher. His English
teacher turns out to be a homosexual who tries to bed down
with the young boy, and Holden Caulfield, in the last chapter,
is in a mental institution. Mighty man. How the mighty have
fallen! Picasso, with that fantastic nonsense which he dares to
call art, is, in one sense, an artist of our time far more than any
other, for he dramatically and accurately reflects the mood of
modern man, who, like Willy Loman in *Death of a Salesman*,
neither knows who he is nor where he is going. Picasso's absurd abstractions, with an arm growing out of an ear, with a
breast in the middle of the forehead, with a forehead with one
eye or three eyes or no eyes, in their own way shout out that
modern man is shattered and beyond repair, a lost and lonely
creature. The "God is dead" theologians who point to science
and praise it for revealing the enchanting dimensions of emerg-

ing man in one sense do not even know what modern science is saying.

Who is to claim that every scientific advance has shrunk God and has made man bigger? The opposite can equally well be argued: for every major breakthrough of science, man has not grown but has shrunk. Copernicus, in one sense the father of modern interplanetary space travel, thanks to the new comprehension of the universe he unfolded, certainly did not enlarge man. He made man shrink. Before him, the Western world knew that there was motion upstairs on the heavenly scene. Who could deny it? We could see the stars move, the sun cross the heavens, the moon rise and fall. Of course there was motion. But men believed that the earth was the center of the universe; the earth stood still and all else revolved around it. Man was at the very core of the cosmos, the center of all that was. And then along came Copernicus, who said that the sun stood still and the earth revolved around it. Man was not the center of the universe but instead the frail inhabitant of a whirling ball of mud, pockmarked with pits of hate and war, hurtling through emptiness, living on the very fringe of the universe, not a giant but a midget, an insignificant shrunken soul.

Latent in Darwinism, and as equally open to elaboration and exploration as the idea of man as an emerging giant, was the conviction that man was but an animal, a passing stage in the unfolding and as yet incomplete drama of evolution. Darwinism did not magnify man, make him a giant, for it denied man, reducing him to an accidental product of a mechanical and yet unended progress. Man was not quite even unique— only a link in a chain still being forged.

If Darwin was the greatest name in the natural sciences of a century ago, the greatest name in the social sciences in the twentieth century is Sigmund Freud, the father of modern psychiatry. And Freud too made man shrink even farther. What he said in effect was that man was like an iceberg. Everyone knows what an iceberg is like. The mass of it is below the surface, out of sight, beneath the water. Only a small part of it is visible on top, in clear view. Man's mind is like that. Only a small part of our mind is conscious. The bulk of man's activity is below, out of sight, down in the depths of the subconscious or unconscious. Modern man who prides himself on being a rational, self-determining creature is not that at all! Most of his decisions are not made logically, on the surface, by his conscious mind. They are not *decisions* at all! Instead, his actions are formed down there in the depths of the iceberg by processes man neither comprehends nor controls. Darwin denied man's uniqueness. Freud denied man's self-determining powers. Science's advances did not shrink God and make man large.

To all these things—to the incredible war, to the disasters that followed it and continue to mount up, to the shrinking process unleashed by modern science, to all these things the reaction against earlier liberal optimism points. Man can hurl manned rockets toward the moon, but the rest of us, left behind, dig holes in the ground and call them bomb shelters, seeking, by burrowing into the earth like blind moles, to escape the extinction that hangs over our heads. No wonder George Orwell saw the rise of technology as the most chillingly dehumanizing factor ever to explode on the human scene. No wonder Camus and Sartre pointed to the cosmos and called it absurd. No wonder the modern conservative looks not only with contempt but with amazed pity on the "God is dead" theologian, insisting that he knows not the world in which we live nor modern man who lives therein. Man is not a giant but a little creature faced by awesome foes who threaten to sweep over him. The literature of despair that is on all sides of us is but a literary reflection of the society in which man finds himself, a society that renders him faceless and apparently irrelevant. We live in our tract homes, carbon copies of the man next door. He wears gray flannel too. We wander through our maze of electric wires and concrete canyons, reduced no longer to a number but to a hole in an IBM card, the ultimate expression of nothingness.

To all these things the reaction against an earlier optimism points, insisting that man is in need of more than a good example. Man is in need of a Savior! Not a human exemplar but a divine deliverer, else all is lost.

The reaction goes on to argue that men like Bultmann have not only misunderstood the temper of modern man, but they have also perverted the very message that could have given hope. Bultmann, as we saw, tried to restructure the original message, changing not its content but only its form. In actual fact, however, demythologizing has done both. It has changed not only the language of the original message but the original message as well. What emerges out of Bultmann's demythologizing Christianity is not a liberated or a reformed Christianity, but rather an emasculated, crippled, truncated Christianity, a pitifully impoverished caricature of what was originally there. Bultmann's intentions may have been noble, but his results were disastrous. What emerges from his program is a Jesus who is human and human alone and a view of man that sees him as free and unfettered and solely responsible for his own decisions and salvation. Bultmann takes up that half of the Biblical message which sees man as free and sets aside the other complementary insistence that man is enslaved. When he translates demonology into contemporary psychological vocabulary, he reduces all evil to existential bad intentions. Man is *not,* says Bultmann, interfered with by external forces, either good or bad. All impulses toward good or evil originate within man and are controllable by man.

Here Bultmann is not leading but following, taking up the point of view promulgated by an earlier optimistic anthropology. He would make of man a self-contained unit, bearing in his own person both the seeds of his own problems and the solutions to those problems. Modern depth psychiatry, to which Bultmann is indebted, proceeds on the assumption that locked up in man himself are all the ills and answers. I have this bad tic; my shoulder is bothered by muscle spasms. So the psychiatrist lays me down on his leather-covered couch in his oak-paneled office and probes my past, and finally we discover that I twitch like this because, while my mother was carrying me in the womb the phonograph was playing too loudly and she fell down the stairs (landing on her shoulder), and I have been so frightened ever since that I tremble all over in the clavicular area. Knowing that, knowing the *cause* of my problem, it is just assumed that I have the *answer* to my problem. There is no need to look outside my psyche or my environment to find either cause or solution. Man's ills are not caused by demons, and man's answers will not be produced by divine intervention.

Nowhere in contemporary psychology textbooks will you find a chapter, no matter how the language might be formulated, which deals with the role of evil forces outside man thrusting themselves in, nor will you find a chapter on divine grace, on supernatural intervention, on the renewing power of the Holy Spirit. The vertical has been lost. It is a one-dimensional anthropology. It is truncated and incomplete. It turns man back on himself, tells him to try harder, to make greater resolves, to renew his efforts. The psychologist lays me flat on my back and tells me to talk about *myself*, to probe my own background. But that was my problem in the first place! I already think too much of myself! There simply is no such thing as an inferiority complex. All of us are overly concerned with self. That is our problem, and like Narcissus of old who was enamored of his own reflected image in the pool, we lean over to embrace ourselves and we drown. There is simply no such thing as an inferiority complex. A pimply-faced girl trembles at the doorway to the high school prom. She has an inferiority complex, she says. She is afraid to go in for fear the music will stop and every eye in the room will swivel around to examine her acne. She'll *die* of embarrassment if she has to go in! What makes *her* think *she* is so important that the whole room of dancing people is going to stop and watch *her* walk in? That is not an inferiority complex. That is deep and psychopathic concern for self—the basic problem of us all. And the psychologist tells me to talk about *myself!*

Jesus does not insist: "Talk about yourself!" He insists, "Deny yourself!" The basic Christian thrust has always been to turn man *away* from his own isolated little existence, to lift up his eyes from his own shoestrings and force his gaze upward and outward to the great horizons of God, a power outside himself. Bultmann and the "God is dead" theologians pervert, poison, and pollute the Christian message when they trumpet the absurdity that man is sufficient unto his own needs.

Where do we go from here? Again we have two contrary and opposed points of view. The liberal or modern position argues that man is free and unfettered, a responsible creature who should turn to Jesus as model and this alone will be sufficient. The modern movement, influenced by the positive accomplishments of science, argues that man has great potential for good. On the other hand is the reaction, the insistence that man is indeed helpless and enslaved no matter how we may wish to define the powers that enslave him.

Where do we go from here? Bultmann argues that if we do not demythologize we are dead, for we lose our audience. Modern man will not listen to our message. However, the reaction argues that if we *do* demythologize, then we are already dead, for although we may gain or retain an audience, we have lost the message of liberation which we earlier had to give. Where to from here?

The answer is the answer we have given so often. It is not—it cannot be—a case of either/or. There is something in this swirling diversity of opinion which is valid on both sides. There *is* a sense in which modern science has put at our disposition enormous power and potential. There *is* a sense in which man is responsible and called to account and summoned to behave even as Jesus would. The human model of Jesus is never outdated or irrelevant because he was and is a *human* model. The struggle of man to move ahead, to deal with ills, to roll up his sleeves and perfect vaccines and conquer slums and end wars and employ the devices and insights of the social and natural sciences that can lessen suffering in our day is a process that must never end if man is to call himself a man at all.

But, in this quest, the other side must always also be borne in mind. There are limits and pitfalls. Humility instead of pride is demanded. Every great scientific advance is not in and of itself good, beneficial. Progress is not automatic. Today's joy is tomorrow's sorrow. Education is a neuter; it can be demonic as well as beneficial. A step forward is a step backward. We end one evil, seek to give the Negro his God-ordained rights as a true human being, and we take a step forward. The result is chaos, anarchy, rioting in the streets. Does this mean that the good step forward should never have been taken? To conclude that is to be demonic in the fullest sense. *Of course* that forward step was to be taken. But we must recognize that even as we struggle and try and inch our way forward we are simultaneously hurled backward. Every progress has its regression. Every solution creates its new dilemma. Today's wisdom is tomorrow's despair. Those who would stress solely and exclusively man's capacity for good are naïve and blind to the equally powerful fact of man's capacity for evil—his refusal to walk the path pointed out to him, and more, his inability to move to perfection. He is born in the image of God and sold into the bondage of the devil. One without the other is naïve; the other without the first is despair. Jesus is not only human model but also divine deliverer.

The problem that Bultmann put in front of us—how to interpret the dimension of the demonic in terms that make sense to modern man—remains a problem. He is undoubtedly right in insisting adamantly and often eloquently that contemporary man will not accept this quaint figure painted red and armed with a pitchfork. But, to be exact, *that is not the Biblical picture!* That is the caricature which arose in later centuries of the church. All that the Bible does say, and on this it insists, is that there is some dimension of evil, of tragedy-inflicting powers, independent of man and opposed to God. Man is not the answer to all his own problems, nor even the cause of them all. Ingrained in the very substance of man, and part of the world in which he lives, is not only the mark of God but the power of evil, a negating, denying, destroying power that makes mockery of our highest hopes and most flaming and far-flung aspirations.

But the Christian message is not essentially a negative one of despair counseling resignation. It is positive. It is the electrifying announcement that man is not alone! His dignity, his worth, his value, his ineffable and ineffacable glory is that God *is* and God *cares!* Here is the ultimate measure of man that pulls the arm out of the ear, erases the breast from the middle of the forehead, and restores man to his rightful dimensions. Like Willy Loman, *we* may not always know who we are, but *God* knows. He knows our frail and feeble frame, ripped by weakness, filled with power, paradoxically able and unable. When we stumble, he picks us up. When we stand, he urges us on. When we are guilty, he forgives. When we rebel, he reconciles. When we are helpless, he promises freedom. He sets us partially free here, fully free there. The Kingdom of God is with us now; it is yet to come.

The paradoxical many-splendored grandeur of the dialectical Christian faith speaks to all our problems, answers all our needs, encourages us to use our resources. It gives us the courage and the confidence to tread the paths that by ourselves we could never follow.